Dinosaurs
& Other
Prehistoric
Animals

By TOM McGOWEN

Illustrated by ROD RUTH

CHECKERBOARD PRESS ❖ NEW YORK

Distributed by Funk & Wagnalls, Inc.
Ramsey, New Jersey

Pages 8 through 59:

**Illustrations prepared under the direction of
Dr. Rainer Zangerl
Chairman, Department of Geology
Field Museum of Natural History
Chicago, Illinois**

**Text reviewed and authenticated by
Dr. Dale Russell
Chief, Palaeontology Division
National Museum of Natural Sciences
Ottawa, Ontario, Canada**

Pages 60 through 92:

**Text and illustrations reviewed and
authenticated by Dr. William Turnbull
Curator of Fossil Mammals
Field Museum of Natural History
Chicago, Illinois**

Contents

Dinosaurs—THE TERRIBLE LIZARDS

IN A THICK tangle of forest on the edge of a small lake, an oddly shaped, rather clumsy-looking animal shuffles about in search of food. It has a large, bulky body, a long, thick tail, and a surprisingly small head on the end of a long neck.

As the animal moves about through the foliage, it walks upright on its two, stout back legs, holding its smaller front legs in front of its chest, like arms. Its feet are five-toed, with blunt claws on the toes; its forefeet are much like hands, with four fingers and a large thumb.

When the creature spies a clump of leafy plants growing close to the ground, it drops to all fours and begins munching leaves with its blunt teeth. From nose to tip of tail this plant-eating animal is 20 feet long —about twice as long as an African elephant.

Suddenly, another animal emerges from the forest. It, too, walks upright, but its neck is much shorter and its head much bigger than the plant eater's. Its mouth bristles with sharp teeth.

With a single bound this animal hurls itself upon the plant eater, sinking its teeth into the other's neck. The plant eater strug-

8

BRACHIOSAURUS

Rhamphorhynchus

gles but is quickly subdued. The sharp-toothed creature begins to rip chunks of flesh from the quivering body.

These two creatures were dinosaurs—Plateosaurus, a plant eater, and Teratosaurus, a flesh eater. They lived in Europe about 180 million years ago, and they were just two of the many kinds of strange creatures that hunted and fought and roamed everywhere in the world during the time that is called the Age of Reptiles. Dinosaurs were kings of the world then, as common as people are now. There were dinosaurs with horns, dinosaurs with arm-

ALLOSAURUS

Plateosaurus

ored bodies, and dinosaurs with duckbills. There were dinosaurs that were the biggest land animals that have ever lived and dinosaurs that were no bigger than chickens.

Just what were these strange animals? The name *dinosaur* means "terrible lizard." But dinosaurs were not lizards. And only the big flesh-eating dinosaurs could really be called "terrible." Most kinds of dinosaurs were plant eaters and were really no more terrible than the giraffe or buffalo or other wild animal of today.

The dinosaurs were, of course, reptiles. This means they belong to the same scaly-skinned, cold-blooded family as lizards, snakes, alligators, crocodiles, and turtles. But dinosaurs were quite different from all these other reptiles. There is nothing like a dinosaur living in the world today.

What made the dinosaurs different from other reptiles? It wasn't size, because although many dinosaurs were giants, some of them were no bigger than many lizards, snakes, and crocodiles living now. And it wasn't their strange appearance, because many of today's reptiles are every bit as odd-looking as any of the dinosaurs were.

The main thing that made dinosaurs so different from today's living reptiles is the way their bodies were constructed. Nearly every reptile now living, except for snakes and legless lizards, walks on four legs that sprawl out from the sides of its body. But the first kinds of dinosaurs were all *two-legged* animals that walked and ran on their back legs (as we do) and used their smaller front legs like arms. Even the four-legged dinosaurs were really just two-legged animals that walked on all fours because their bodies were too big and bulky for only two legs to carry.

Of course, it took many millions of years for two-legged dinosaurs to turn into four-legged ones. And that's an important fact to remember about dinosaurs—they didn't all live at the same time. There were dinosaurs living in this world for 130 million years, and many kinds of dinosaurs lived millions of years apart from each other. In fact, some of the dinosaurs we know about were *ancestors* of some of the other dinosaurs!

Nearly everything we know about dinosaurs has been learned from fossils. Fossils are records of plant and animal life that have been preserved in stone. For example, dinosaurs walked in mud and left footprints, and the mud hardened into stone with the footprints still in it. From such prints scientists can tell how dinosaurs walked and ran. Many dinosaur bones and skeletons that turned to stone over millions of years have been found. From them, scientists can tell how big a dinosaur was, how much it weighed, what it ate, and sometimes even how well it could see, hear, and smell. Prints of dinosaur skin and even petrified "mummies" of dinosaurs have been found, telling us much about what dinosaurs looked like. Even petrified dinosaur eggs have been found, solving the mystery of how dinosaur babies were born.

New fossils and new ways of learning things from fossils are being found all the time, adding to our knowledge of dino-

Snake

Turtle

Tortoise

Lizard

Present-day Reptiles

Alligator

Crocodile

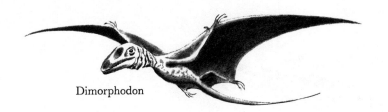

Dimorphodon

saurs. Sometimes these discoveries show us that what we had thought to be true about certain dinosaurs is all wrong. Sometimes dinosaurs even have to be renamed—which is why, if you've read about dinosaurs before, you may be surprised to find some old friends with new names in this book.

Remember, then, that dinosaurs were reptiles—but not like any reptiles that are living today—and that they didn't all live at the same time. Here's a list that will help you understand just when each kind of prehistoric animal you'll read about in this book was alive.

200 MILLION TO 180 MILLION YEARS AGO

Coelophysis	(see-loh-FY-ses)
Plateosaurus	(PLAD-ee-uh-SAW-ruhs)
Proganochelys	(proh-GAN-oh-CHEL-eez)
Teratosaurus	(ter-AT-uh-SAW-ruhs)
Trilophosaurus	(try-LOH-fuh-SAW-ruhs)

180 MILLION TO 160 MILLION YEARS AGO

Megalosaurus	(MEG-uh-loh-SAW-ruhs)
Scelidosaurus	(SEL-uh-doh-SAW-ruhs)

160 MILLION TO 135 MILLION YEARS AGO

Allosaurus	(AL-uh-SAW-ruhs)
Apatosaurus	(uh-PAT-uh-SAW-ruhs)
Archaeopteryx	(AHR-kee-AHP-tuh-riks)
Brachiosaurus	(BRAK-ee-oh-SAW-ruhs)
Camarasaurus	(KAM-uh-ruh-SAW-ruhs)
Camptosaurus	(KAMP-tuh-SAW-ruhs)
Ceratosaurus	(seh-RAT-uh-SAW-ruhs)
Chialingosaurus	(chy-uh-LING-uh-SAW-ruhs)
Compsognathus	(kahmp-SAHG-nuh-thuhs)
Dapedius	(duh-PEE-dee-uhs)
Dimorphodon	(dy-MOHR-foh-dahn)
Diplodocus	(dih-ploh-DAHK-uhs)

Kentrosaurus	(KENT-ruh-SAW-ruhs)
Omosaurus	(OH-muh-SAW-ruhs)
Ornitholestes	(awr-NITH-uh-LEH-steez)
Rhamphorhynchus	(RAM-fuh-RING-kuhs)
Stegosaurus	(STEG-uh-SAW-ruhs)
Theriosuchus	(thehr-ee-oh-SOO-kuhs)

135 MILLION TO 100 MILLION YEARS AGO

Acanthopholis	(ah-KAN-thuh-FOHL-is)
Hypsilophodon	(HIP-suh-LAHF-uh-dahn)
Iguanodon	(eh-GWAHN-uh-dahn)
Polacanthus	(POHL-uh-KAN-thuhs)
Pterodactylus	(TERR-uh-DAK-teh-luhs)

100 MILLION TO 70 MILLION YEARS AGO

Albertosaurus	(al-BER-tuh-SAW-ruhs)
Anatosaurus	(uh-NAT-uh-SAW-ruhs)
Ankylosaurus	(ANG-kih-loh-SAW-ruhs)
Chasmosaurus	(CHAS-muh-SAW-ruhs)
Corythosaurus	(kuh-RITH-uh-SAW-ruhs)
Euoplocephalus	(yoo-uh-pluh-SEF-uh-luhs)
Hesperornis	(HES-puh-RAWR-nehs)
Kritosaurus	(KRY-tuh-SAW-ruhs)
Lambeosaurus	(LAM-bee-uh-SAW-ruhs)
Monoclonius	(MAHN-uh-KLOH-nee-uhs)
Nodosaurus	(NOHD-uh-SAW-ruhs)
Ornithomimus	(awr-NITH-uh-MY-muhs)
Pachycephalosaurus	(PAK-ee-SEF-al-uh-SAW-ruhs)
Pachyophis	(pak-ee-OH-fuhs)
Paleoscincus	(PAE-lee-uh-SKINK-us)
Parasaurolophus	(par-uh-sawr-AHL-uh-fuhs)
Pentaceratops	(PEN-tuh-SERR-uh-tahps)
Phobosuchus	(foh-boh-SOOK-uhs)
Pinacosaurus	(pyn-AK-uh-SAW-ruhs)
Protoceratops	(PROH-doh-SERR-uh-tahps)
Pteranodon	(tuh-RAN-uh-dahn)
Spinosaurus	(SPYN-uh-SAW-ruhs)
Struthiomimus	(STROO-thee-oh-MY-muhs)
Styracosaurus	(sty-RAK-uh-SAW-ruhs)
Titanosaurus	(ty-TAN-uh-SAW-ruhs)
Torosaurus	(TOH-roh-SAW-ruhs)
Triceratops	(try-SERR-uh-tahps)
Tyrannosaurus	(teh-RAN-uh-SAW-ruhs)

Tyrannosaurus Rex

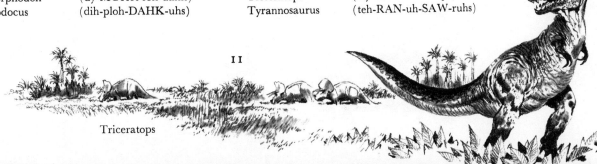

Triceratops

Coelophysis—ONE OF THE FIRST

THE WAVES of a great green sea surged and swelled and came rolling in with a hiss upon a red, sandy shore. The land stretched away from the shore, low and flat, crossed by many lazily flowing rivers and dotted with shallow lakes. No grass or flowers covered the red soil, but there were clumps of ferns everywhere, and the riverbanks were choked with thick clusters of 15-foot-high rushes.

The land rose gradually, and on the high ground dense forests sprawled. Trees with lacy clusters of fan-shaped leaves grew in the forests, together with stubby, treelike plants that had trunks shaped like balls and barrels, crowned with circles of feathery leaves. Farther inland on the higher ground the black, pointed snouts of volcanoes poked up at the sky. From time to time one of them might rumble sullenly and spout spumes of black smoke into the air. And sometimes one of them would explode into fiery fury, and for days the sun would be blotted out by dark, drifting clouds of ash.

This was the western part of the North American continent—180 million years ago.

A great many kinds of animals crept and crawled and skittered and slogged about on the red flatlands and in the forests. In the wet places there were short-tailed, four-footed creatures that looked somewhat like lizards but were really amphibians. Dragonflies were numerous, and roaches and spiders swarmed everywhere, looking much the same as they do today and doing much the same sorts of things they do now. There were no ants, bees, or butterflies though, nor would there be for many millions of years. But there were tiny, furry, ratlike creatures that darted and dashed about in the underbrush. They were ancestors of the mammals. There were also birdlike creatures.

And there were plenty of cold-blooded, scaly-skinned reptiles. In fact, there were so many reptiles in the world that scientists call this period the Age of Reptiles—an age that lasted 130 million years!

Many of those reptiles of long ago resembled some of the kinds of reptiles that are living now. There were turtles, much like the turtles of today except that those ancient turtles couldn't pull their heads and legs all the way into their shells. There were lots of lizards. And there were small beasts that looked like snub-nosed croco-

Dragonfly

Spider

Proganochelys

COELOPHYSIS

Trilophosaurus

Williamsonia

diles, and large beasts that looked like long-nosed crocodiles.

But there were some reptiles that were very different from all the others. While most reptiles waddle about on all fours, these creatures walked and ran upright on their two back legs. They were the first kinds of the creatures we now call dinosaurs.

Some of the early dinosaurs were big, bulky creatures, such as Plateosaurus, which lived in what is now Germany. Others were small and slim and ran swiftly, with body bent forward and long neck and tail stretched out stiffly. Dinosaurs such as these were common in North America 180 million years ago.

Scientists have named one such American dinosaur Coelophysis. They know a lot about it from some marvelously well-preserved fossil skeletons found in New Mexico. Even though Coelophysis was a dinosaur and the word *dinosaur* means "terrible lizard," Coelophysis probably wouldn't seem very terrible if you saw it running about in a zoo. We think of dinosaurs as being huge. But Coelophysis, like most of the first kinds of dinosaurs, was rather small. It was only about 8 feet long, and nearly half of that length was tail. It was about 3 feet tall standing upright, and no more than 2 feet tall when it ran because of the way it bent its body forward. It was slender and birdlike, with hollow bones like the bones of a bird. *Coelophysis* means "hollow form," referring to these bones. It weighed only 40 or 50 pounds—not much more than an average eight-year-old child.

These little dinosaurs probably lived in large groups, like bird flocks. Such flocks must have terrorized the many kinds of small reptiles that lived near them on the red New Mexico flatlands. For Coelophysis was a flesh eater, and the flesh it ate was torn in chunks from the bodies of animals it hunted and caught. It probably ate any small animal that wasn't fast enough to get away or well armored enough to be safe from its sharp, little teeth. There's even some evidence that Coelophysis was a cannibal and sometimes feasted on young animals of its own kind, as many snakes, crocodiles, and other reptiles do today.

We can tell that Coelophysis was a flesh eater by looking at the teeth in its fossil skull. Those teeth are small, but they're as sharp as daggers, and they have saw-toothed edges, like the cutting edge of a steak knife. Coelophysis's front legs also show that it was a flesh eater. They are little arms with four-fingered hands, and on three of the fingers are sharp claws. Coelophysis could close its hands, which means that it probably used them for grabbing things. It may have held its prey with those little clawed hands while the knifelike teeth did their job of cutting the animal to pieces. If you've ever seen a picture of an eagle or owl or other bird of prey holding a rat or rabbit in its claws as it tears into the flesh with its beak, you can easily imagine how Coelophysis must have looked as it was having dinner.

Coelophysis's back legs were completely different from the front ones. They were

14

Cycad

almost exactly like the legs of a bird. The feet had three toes with sharp claws on them, much like the feet of many modern birds. Footprints of three-toed dinosaurs have been found in many parts of the world. They were made when dinosaurs trudged or trotted through thick mud that hardened into rock over many millions of years. Some of these footprints are just about the size of Coelophysis's feet and may have been made by some of these active, little dinosaurs. Mixed in with the footprints is an occasional print of a dinosaur's bottom, which seems to show that when Coelophysis got tired it probably sat down to rest on its tail, much as kangaroos do today. Coelophysis might even have slept in a sitting-down position.

From footprints in rock and from fossil skeletons we have been able to learn a lot about Coelophysis and other dinosaurs. But there are some things that bones and footprints just can't tell us. They can't tell us what color Coelophysis or any other dino-saur might have been. Coelophysis may have been brightly colored, as many small lizards and snakes are today. Or it may have been dull green or brown, as many alligators and crocodiles are. We are pretty sure that the dinosaurs saw things in color, as we do, and some of them may have had patterns of color on their skins that helped them blend into the vegetation and hide from their enemies. But we don't know this for sure.

And we don't know whether Coelophysis or any other dinosaur made noises. It might have hissed, as many snakes and lizards do. It might have croaked or grunted or bellowed. It might have screeched like a big bird. Or maybe dinosaurs couldn't make any noise at all.

We don't know these things and we probably never shall. For no human ever saw or heard a live dinosaur and never will. The last dinosaurs were all dead and gone more than 60 million years before man's earliest ancestors came shuffling into the world.

Apatosaurus — THE HARMLESS GIANT

THE AIR shimmers with heat above a small, shallow lake. Dragonflies dart and dodge about. From time to time there's a sudden splash, followed by a spread of ripples over the blue-green water as some strange, square-scaled fish hurls itself out of the water to gulp a passing insect in midair.

In the shallow water near the shore an animal is silently standing. It is simply enormous! Its huge, bulky body is supported by four massive legs as thick as old tree trunks. Now it shuffles ponderously up onto the bank, and the ground seems to shiver under the tread of those giant, barrellike feet. The creature's snaky neck is as long as a boa constrictor's whole body, and when it lifts that long neck up to peer suspiciously about, its blunt head is higher than most of the nearby trees!

Giant long-necked, long-tailed creatures such as this were the biggest of all the dinosaurs and the biggest animals that have ever lumbered upon the land. They were plant eaters that walked on four legs, and we call them the sauropod dinosaurs.

One of the best known of these sauropods is the dinosaur that many people called

Brontosaurus. But that isn't its right name. Scientists call it *Apatosaurus,* which means "unreal lizard" or "untrue lizard."

Perhaps Apatosaurus got its name because the scientist who found it couldn't believe it was real! From the end of its lengthy tail to the tip of its nose, Apatosaurus was about 70 feet long—almost as long as a whole passenger coach on a railroad train. It was about 15 feet high at the shoulder and weighed as much as five full-grown elephants. It was a living, moving mountain of bone, flesh, and muscle!

When fossil skeletons of Apatosaurus and other giant sauropods were first found, scientists felt that such enormous, bulky creatures were probably far too heavy to have been able to walk on land—their legs could not have supported the weight of their big bodies. It was believed that Apatosaurus and other sauropods probably spent most of their lives in lakes and rivers, where the water would have helped support their great weight. Apatosaurus appears to have had rather weak teeth, so it was thought that these big animals fed mostly on soft plants that grew in water or at the water's edge.

Another reason that reinforced the belief

Rhamphorhynchus

16

APATOSAURUS

Rhamphorhynchus

that sauropods were water dwellers was the location of their nostrils—not at the tip of the snout, where those of most land animals are, but up on the top of the head, like the nostrils of whales and dolphins. It seemed that a sauropod could have stood in very deep water that covered its entire body and breathed by stretching its neck so that the nostrils on its head were just poking above the surface.

There is also some positive evidence that sauropods spent time in the water. Fossil footprints of sauropod feet plodding over the muddy bottom of a swamp have been found, as have footprints made by a sauropod that was probably swimming in a lake and putting its front feet down from time to time to push itself along.

Today, some scientists still feel that sauropods probably were mostly water dwellers. But other scientists disagree. They believe that sauropods such as Apatosaurus were land animals. Footprints have been found of a herd of sauropods that walked over the ground close together, with the small young ones in the middle and the biggest ones on the outside as guards. This offers evidence that sauropods were quite at home on land. These scientists also point out that a sauropod's feet were much like the feet of an elephant: broad and flat and constructed to support the weight of a big, heavy land animal. It also appears that sauropod teeth really were strong enough to chew tough leaves. Thus, these scientists think that Apatosaurus and other sauropods were land dwellers that lived much as elephants do today—in herds that moved

about browsing on tree leaves. The long necks of sauropods would have been a great help in reaching the tops of trees for leaves, and it's possible that some sauropods were able to reach even higher by rearing up on their hind legs and using their tails to brace themselves.

As for the nostrils of sauropods, which most scientists once thought couldn't be anything but the nostrils of a water dweller, some scientists now have a new idea. They point out that there are several kinds of land animals now living that have such nostrils above the tops of their heads—elephants and tapirs, which have *trunks*. So, these scientists say, perhaps sauropods, too, had trunks! That would have enabled them to reach even higher.

Apatosaurus had neither sharp claws nor sharp teeth, and was apparently very slow-moving. However, it was probably well able to defend itself against a faster, sharp-toothed flesh eater such as Allosaurus. A whipping blow of its huge powerful tail could have sent a smaller dinosaur sprawling, with broken bones. It may also have been able to defend itself by rearing up and plunging down at a smaller creature to crush it. Allosaurus may have trailed sauropod herds in the hope of seizing a stray young one or an old, sick adult, but they might not have tried to attack a full-grown, healthy sauropod.

Many kinds of these giant creatures lived together on the prehistoric lowland plains, just as many kinds of antelope now live on the plains of Africa. Some sauropods were bigger than others, and some had more

18

Diplodocus

teeth than others, but they were all shaped the same way. They all had big bodies and long, long necks and tails. And, like Apatosaurus, they all had their nostrils on the tops of their heads.

One of the smallest sauropods was Saltosaurus, which was only about 40 feet long. Saltosaurus's back and sides were covered with armor formed of thousands of hard knobs and disks of bone imbedded in the skin. This may have prevented flesh eaters from biting or clawing Saltosaurus's back.

One of the longest sauropods was Diplodocus, which was nearly 90 feet long. Despite its greater length, however, Diplodocus weighed much less than Apatosaurus because it was much less bulky.

Probably the biggest sauropods and the biggest of all dinosaurs were the giant brachiosaurs. They were different from Apatosaurus and other sauropods in that their front legs were longer than their back ones; they were shaped much like the giraffes of today. Brachiosaurus, one of the best-known brachiosaurs, was about 75 feet long, and its head reared 40 feet into the air. But some remains of even bigger brachiosaurs have been found: creatures that have been nicknamed "supersaurus" and "ultrasaurus." Ultrasaurus may have been more than 100 feet long!

Apparently not even Ultrasaurus was the very biggest dinosaur. A dinosaur named Antarctosaurus may also have been more than 100 feet long. Recently scientists found some bones of a sauropod that has been named *Seismosaurus*, meaning "earth-shaker lizard," which may have been as much as 120 feet long. And some sauropod footprints found in Morocco seem to have been made by a creature that was more than 150 feet long! No doubt about it, the sauropod dinosaurs were truly giants!

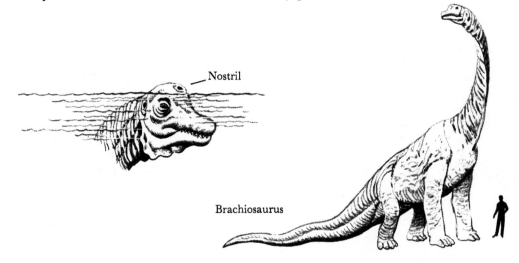

Nostril

Brachiosaurus

Comparative Size of a Six-foot Man

19

Stegosaurus—THE ROOFED DINOSAUR

ALL THE DINOSAURS were strange-looking creatures. But surely the strangest of all was Stegosaurus, a dinosaur that lived in North America about 150 million years ago.

For one thing, when you look at a picture of Stegosaurus or at its fossil skeleton, you wonder how such a big animal could have such a tiny head. Stegosaurus's body was about 20 feet long and weighed about 2 tons, but its narrow, birdlike head was only 16 inches long. The brain in that head weighed only about 2 ounces and was no bigger than a walnut.

For another thing, Stegosaurus's back legs were more than twice as long as its front ones. Thus, while its nose was nearly touching the ground, its rear end was nearly 8 feet in the air. No other dinosaur was quite as oddly shaped.

Lastly, and perhaps the strangest feature of all, along Stegosaurus's back and down most of its tail marched a row of bony plates that looked like the spades in a deck of playing cards. The plates on Stegosaurus's neck were small, but they got bigger the farther back they went, with those at the hips being 2 feet high. Each plate was about

2 inches thick and covered with tough, horny skin.

Stegosaurus gets its name from these strange bony plates. Professor O. C. Marsh, who first discovered fossils of Stegosaurus, felt that the bony plates looked like roof shingles. So he gave the animal its name, which means "roofed lizard."

For a hundred years, those pointed plates on Stegosaurus's back presented scientists with two perplexing puzzles. One puzzle was, just how did the plates *fit* on the animal's back? The plates weren't attached to Stegosaurus's skeleton, so whenever a fossil skeleton was found, the plates were always separate and often jumbled, and there seemed no sure way to tell how they had been arranged.

The scientist who found the very first Stegosaurus skeleton fossil, in 1886, was sure the plates must have run in a single row along the animal's back. But later, other scientists began to disagree with this assumption. Part of the skeleton's tail was missing and they thought some of the plates might be missing, too. They finally decided there were probably twice as many plates as had been found, and so there wouldn't have

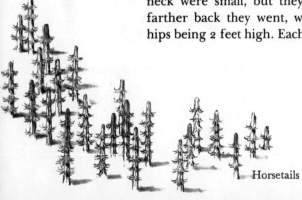

Horsetails

Ceratosaurus

STEGOSAURUS

been room for just a single row—there must have been two rows, arranged in pairs.

But this caused a problem. No two of the plates were the same size, which meant they couldn't have been in pairs because one of the plates in each pair would have been completely different from the other. No animal in the world is built like that, with something on one side of its body that is different from what's on the other side. So scientists decided the plates couldn't have been in pairs, they must have run down Stegosaurus's back in a zigzag pattern—a small plate on the left, then a little bigger one on the right, and so on. But many scientists felt this was a rather odd arrangement, and really weren't sure about it.

Then, in 1986, it was discovered that the first scientist had been right after all! There were only 17 plates on Stegosaurus's back, and not 34 as other scientists had later come to believe, and the 17 plates fit in a single row. So that puzzle was solved.

The second puzzle was, what were those bony plates on Stegosaurus's back *for*? Over the years, scientists had a great many different ideas about them, but most scientists now think they were a way of helping Stegosaurus get warm quickly. Apparently, there were big veins in the plates, and if a Stegosaurus stood so that the row of plates was facing the sun, the plates would have soon grown hot and the blood passing through them would have carried warmth throughout the animal's body. This would have been very useful if Stegosaurus was a cold-blooded creature as all reptiles of today are—it would have been able to warm up quicker and move easily, instead of staying stiff and slow after a cool night.

However, some scientists think the row of hard, pointed bony plates was a means of defense. They might have helped keep a meat-eating dinosaur from jumping on Stegosaurus's back. Perhaps Stegosaurus was able to point them toward the side from which a meat eater was attacking.

Stegosaurus's tail was 10 feet long—about half the length of the animal's whole body. It was a thick, powerful tail, and sticking up from the end of it were two pairs of enormous, hornlike spikes, each nearly a yard long. Maybe we don't know for sure what Stegosaurus's bony back plates were for, but there's not much doubt about what those big spikes were for. Stegosaurus's tail was a war club!

It's easy to imagine how the ancient reptile used its tail to defend itself. Picture a forest filled with feathery-leafed palms and ferns and lacy ginkgo trees. A bulky Stegosaurus is moving among the trees. It stops from time to time to clip a mouthful of greenery from the top of a low-growing plant. Slowly, it makes its way to a clearing through which flows a narrow stream. The big animal lowers its tiny, birdlike head and begins to gulp water.

Suddenly, out of the trees on the other side of the stream stalks a big, two-legged reptile. Its wide mouth bristles with sharp teeth, and the four-fingered hands on its forelegs are tipped with savage talons. On the beast's nose is a stubby horn. A flesh-eating Ceratosaurus!

The flesh eater hurls itself across the

stream, its taloned feet sending up splashes. The stegosaur jerks its head out of the water and clumsily moves away. But it keeps its body twisted around so that its tail is toward the attacking Ceratosaurus.

The Ceratosaurus charges forward. As it does so, the stegosaur swings its tail viciously, slamming it into the flesh eater. The Ceratosaurus is sent staggering, its flank marked with several deep, bloody gashes made by the spikes on the stegosaur's tail! Once more the Ceratosaurus tries to close in and sink its teeth and claws into the stegosaur's flesh. Again a blow from the plant eater's tail knocks the flesh eater reeling, with new bloody welts on its body. Now, moving as quickly as it can, the stegosaur makes its way into the safety of the trees. Dazed and in pain from its frightful wounds, the Ceratosaurus stares after it for a few moments, then limps sullenly off.

Fossil bones of Stegosaurus have been found in North America and England, and bones of Stegosaurus's relatives have been found in many other parts of the world. Kentrosaurus was an African stegosaur that was a little smaller than its American cousin and had fewer bony plates and more spikes on its tail. Chialingosaurus was a stegosaur that lived in eastern Asia. Fossil bones and even some eggs of a stegosaur named Omosaurus have been found in several parts of Europe. All these animals lived at about the same time.

All this tells us that stegosaurs were plentiful in the world of 150 million years ago. Scientists would say that animals that were this widespread were "successful" and should have been around for a long time. And yet, the stegosaurs all died off and vanished many millions of years before any of the other kinds of dinosaurs did. Why this happened we don't know. It's just another one of the many mysteries connected with those most mysterious creatures, the dinosaurs.

Allosaurus — THE HUNTER OF GIANTS

THE FOREST is thick and green and gloomy and silent. The air is hot and damp. Tiny beads of water drip steadily from the little fan-shaped leaves of sweating ginkgo trees and patter softly on the ground. The only sound or movement is the occasional buzz and flash of a winged insect darting through the green shadows.

But then, farther back in the forest, something moves—a huge, two-legged shape among the trees. The sound of its heavy feet padding in the mud breaks the forest silence. The creature moves out of the shadows into a patch of sunlight and stands for a moment, turning its head sharply from side to side as it peers about.

It is a huge, fearful reptile! Its 2½-foot-long head is split by an enormous mouth that seems to grin, showing rows of sharp, curved, 3-inch teeth. Its hands are 3-fingered, and on each finger is a razor-sharp talon. From its nose to the end of its long, powerful tail it is 34 feet long and stands nearly 10 feet high. It is a monstrous, frightening animal, like a dragon in a legend!

This was Allosaurus, the giant flesh-eating dinosaur that roamed the plains and stream beds of western North America about 150 million years ago. Many scientists think it was a fierce killer, ruling its part of the ancient world just as lions and tigers rule their parts of the world now.

Small flesh-eating dinosaurs ate small animals, and big flesh-eating dinosaurs ate big animals. Allosaurus was the biggest flesh-eating dinosaur of its time, and it ate some of the biggest of all animals. Its main source of food was the flesh of the long-necked, 70-foot-long Apatosaurus that weighed as much as several elephants. We know for sure that Allosaurus ate Apatosaurus because fossil Apatosaurus bones have been found with the marks of Allosaurus teeth in them. And at least one Allosaurus, feasting on Apatosaurus flesh, bit so fiercely and hungrily into its prey that some of its teeth broke off! They were found among the Apatosaurus's bones.

Allosauruses may have lived alone most of the time, or they may have lived and hunted in small groups—perhaps a mother and two or three young. A hunting Allosaurus probably prowled along slowly, its body bent forward and tail stretched straight out behind. Sighting prey, it prob-

ALLOSAURUS

24

Apatosaurus

Theriosuchus

Camptosaurus

ably broke into a run. It may not have been able to run very fast or very far without tiring quickly, but it was likely more than quick enough to catch up with a slow-moving sauropod or even a faster creature, such as a Camptosaurus. To make a kill, an Allosaurus probably clamped its savage teeth in its victim's neck, twisting and tearing as it used its clawed hands and feet to rip and tear at the body. It might have taken some time to kill a big sauropod this way, but smaller prey would have been quickly finished off.

To feed, Allosaurus stood with its tail stretched out straight, for balance, and with the top part of its body bent forward so that its clawed hands were resting on the victim's body. The flesh eater sank its teeth into the dead dinosaur and then pulled and tugged and jerked its head until a huge chunk of flesh tore away. Allosaurus gulped such chunks down without chewing. It was able to swallow pieces of meat which were nearly as big as its whole mouth because, like a snake, the bones of its head could come apart slightly so that the whole head stretched.

Some scientists have suggested that Allosaurus didn't really hunt and kill its food, but simply ate dead animals it found as it wandered from place to place. But many scientists think that any animal with teeth and claws as sharp as those of Allosaurus must have been a fierce hunter and killer. And some fossils have been found that certainly seem to show that Allosaurus really did hunt the big Apatosaurus.

These fossils are footprints that were found in a Texas riverbed in 1940. Some of them were made when an Apatosaurus or one of the other gigantic sauropods sloshed along through a shallow stream. Its big feet sank into the mud, leaving clear tracks that hardened into stone over millions of years. And right alongside the sauropod's tracks, pointed in the same direction, are the footprints of an Allosaurus or a big meat-eating dinosaur like it. It seems clear that the Allosaurus *was* hunting the other dinosaur, because where the sauropod's tracks swerve suddenly to the left, so do the Allosaurus's footprints. It looks as if the sauropod, aware that it was being followed by the flesh eater, moved into the middle of the stream, hoping to find deeper water. But the water was still shallow enough for the Allosaurus to keep wading after the big plant eater.

There's no way of telling from these tracks how far apart the two animals were, but they were probably able to see each other. We can imagine the sauropod twisting its long neck to look anxiously back at its pursuer and the Allosaurus splashing along with its horrible, grinning mouth and its clawed hands twitching eagerly. We don't know if the sauropod got away or if the flesh eater finally caught up with it. But isn't it exciting to think about these two huge creatures splashing through that long-ago stream and leaving footprints which lasted more than a hundred million years to tell us the story of that long-ago hunt?

Allosaurus had a smaller cousin that also lived in North America at about the same

26

time and place. It is called Ceratosaurus, and it was 17 feet long and about 8 feet high, with a 20-inch head and 2-inch teeth. It looked like a small Allosaurus except that it had a sort of bony knob above each eye and a short horn on the end of its nose.

Scientists are not quite sure what that horn was for. It wasn't long or sharp enough to be used for killing prey. Many scientists think perhaps the horn was used in fights between Ceratosauruses themselves. Male Ceratosauruses may have used their horns to push and poke at each other in fights over females at mating time, as male deer use their antlers today. They couldn't really injure each other this way, but after a time one would just give up and leave. Female Ceratosauruses probably had no horns.

Allosaurus had other relatives living in many parts of the world. One of these was Megalosaurus, which lived in England and possibly in other parts of Europe as well.

Megalosaurus was smaller than Allosaurus—about 20 feet long and 12 feet high. But otherwise it looked much like its American cousin. It is quite a famous dinosaur among scientists because it was Megalosaurus's fossil bones that were the first dinosaur fossils to be studied, and Megalosaurus was the first dinosaur to be given a name. You might think that the first dinosaur known would have been given a very special, fancy name. But all that *Megalosaurus* means is "large lizard."

And what about Allosaurus? Does this huge, savage monster have a name that's worthy of the most ferocious flesh eater of its time? Not at all! It's hard to imagine why the man who named Allosaurus chose the name he did—for *Allosaurus* means simply "other lizard."

Ceratosaurus

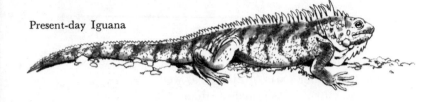

Present-day Iguana

Iguanodon—THE MOST FAMOUS DINOSAUR

THERE WAS once a party held inside a dinosaur!

Of course, it wasn't a real dinosaur. It was a model—a life-size model of a dinosaur called Iguanodon. The model was hollow, and at a table that had been placed inside it, 22 men had a dinner party. The men were all scientists who were interested in dinosaurs, and the party was in honor of the most famous dinosaur of the time—none other than Iguanodon itself.

Iguanodon was famous because it was the first dinosaur that people really knew anything about. Until about 150 years ago, no one knew that there were such things as dinosaurs. People knew about fossil bones and footprints, but they thought that the bones belonged to long-dead elephants or other large animals, and that the footprints had been made by big birds. No one had the slightest idea that giant reptiles had once roamed the world.

Then, one March morning in 1822, Mrs. Gideon Mantell, the wife of an English doctor, went for a walk in the country. As she passed a pile of rocks, something caught her eye. It seemed to be a huge tooth, buried in a piece of rock. Mrs. Mantell picked

up the rock and took it home to show her husband.

Dr. Mantell collected fossils for fun, and he knew a lot about them. But he had never seen anything like this tooth. He couldn't imagine what kind of animal might have had such teeth in its jaws. He began to spend all his spare time searching among the rocks where his wife had found the tooth, hoping to find more fossils from the same animal. His efforts were rewarded, for he found several more teeth and some fossil bones as well.

He showed these fossils to several scientists who told him that the teeth belonged to an ancient rhinoceros and the bones to an extinct hippopotamus. But then he chanced to show the fossil teeth to a man who had spent many years studying the iguana, a lizard of Mexico and Central America.

"Why," said the man, "they look just like an iguana's teeth. Only, they are much, much bigger!"

Dr. Mantell was now sure he had discovered a new kind of animal—a giant plant-eating lizard that had lived many years ago. He named the animal *Iguano-*

don, which means "iguana tooth," and he wrote a description of what he thought it must have been like.

Just about the same time, another scientist published a description of some fossil bones he had been studying. He had decided that they were the bones of a giant flesh-eating lizard (Megalosaurus). Most other scientists agreed with him. And they also agreed that Dr. Mantell's fossils belonged to a different kind of lizard giant that had lived at the same time as the flesh eater. Dinosaurs had been discovered!

Other dinosaur fossils were soon found, and people everywhere became excited and curious about these strange animals of long ago. Scientists began to try to puzzle out what the creatures had looked like, and in 1853 a sculptor with the odd name of Waterhouse Hawkins decided to make a life-size model of a dinosaur. He picked the dinosaur that scientists seemed to know the most about—Dr. Mantell's Iguanodon. And that's how Iguanodon became famous.

The model that Mr. Hawkins built was the very same model in which the 22 scientists had their dinner party. It now stands in a park in the city of London, and people who know a lot about dinosaurs smile when they see it, for it doesn't look much like a dinosaur—it looks like a fat rhinoceros with scales and a long tail. That's because the scientists who first studied dinosaurs thought Iguanodon was simply a giant iguana lizard, and because a short, sharp horn found among some Iguanodon fossils led them to believe that Iguanodon had a horn on its nose. Scientists also thought that

Iguanodon was much bigger than it really was, which is why the model is big enough for 22 men to be able to sit in it.

For many years it was thought that the model showed pretty much how Iguanodon had really looked. Then, in 1877, some coal miners in Belgium made a wonderful discovery. Right where they were digging, a stream had run through a narrow gully millions of years before. Mud, dead plants, and dead animals were carried by the flowing water and piled up all together at places along the riverbank. As the miners dug a new tunnel, they came to just such a place and found the skeletons of 23 dinosaurs. The skeletons were all of the same kind of dinosaur, and scientists soon realized what dinosaurs these creatures had been— iguanodonts!

All those skeletons showed the scientists what Iguanodon had *really* looked like, and it wasn't much like Mr. Hawkins's model. Iguanodon was not a four-footed animal as everyone had thought. It walked upright on its two back legs. And it didn't have a horn on its nose—both of its "thumbs" were horns!

From those skeletons and from fossil footprints and even from prints of skin, we now know more about Iguanodon than we do about most other dinosaurs. It lived about 100 million years ago in what is now England, continental Europe, and North Africa. It was a bulky, good-sized dinosaur that weighed about 7 tons, and was about 15 feet high and more than 30 feet long. As Dr. Mantell had seen by the shape of its teeth, it was a plant eater. Some scientists think it

Ginkgo

may have had a long tongue, like that of a giraffe, with which it pulled twigs into its mouth, snipped the tops off with the sharp, bony front of its jaws, and ground them to a pulp between its rows of teeth.

Iguanodon's hands were much like human hands. Iguanodon probably used them to hold on to the branches from which it was munching leaves. But the thumbs of those hands were short, sharp spikes, like horns, and most scientists think they were used as weapons. Maybe if Iguanodon was attacked by a flesh-eating dinosaur, it used its sharp thumbs like daggers and jabbed them into its enemy's belly!

Although Iguanodon was a big, heavy dinosaur, we can tell from some of its tracks that it could move quite fast if it wanted to. When it ran, it lifted its tail off the ground and bent its body far forward. And from some of the tracks we can see that when Iguanodon got tired it leaned back and sat on its tail.

Iguanodon belonged to a group of dinosaurs that are called *ornithopods,* which means "bird feet." We know a lot about the other dinosaurs in this group—Iguanodon's ancestors and descendants.

Camptosaurus, an American ornithopod that lived many millions of years earlier than Iguanodon, was probably an ancestor. It looked just about like Iguanodon but was much smaller—only averaging about 15 feet long and 7 or 8 feet high. An even smaller ancestor was Hypsilophodon, a dinosaur that looked like an Iguanodon but was only about 5 feet long and 2 feet high.

Some of Iguanodon's descendants were the hadrosaurs, or duck-billed dinosaurs. Another descendant was an extremely odd dinosaur with the jawbreaking name of Pachycephalosaurus. That means "thick-headed lizard," which is a good name because the top of this strange creature's head swelled up into a big bump of solid bone as much as 10 inches thick! And all around this bump, and on the dinosaur's nose, there were clusters of small, bony knobs and spikes.

What could these thick bone heads have been for? It's a puzzle to scientists, because no animal living today has such a head. But maybe these dinosaurs used their thick skulls the same way that billy goats do—maybe they fought with each other at mating time by banging their heads together!

Pachycephalosaurus

Compsognathus — A TINY DINOSAUR

THE VERY WORD "dinosaur" makes most people think of something huge and fearsome. It conjures up thoughts of a gigantic, scaly monster, lumbering through steamy jungles with its head reaching higher than the treetops. But while this description fits some of the dinosaurs, it certainly doesn't fit all of them, for many of the dinosaurs were quite small. One of them, in fact, was actually tiny.

About 150 million years ago, at the same time creatures like 34-foot-long Allosaurus were stalking the swamps in search of a 70-foot-long Apatosaurus, a tiny reptile no bigger than a chicken was also scurrying about among the ginkgoes and cycads. It had a 3-inch-long head on a long, slender neck, and its tail was longer than its head, neck, and body all together. It ran swiftly on its two back legs. This little animal was a dinosaur—one of the smallest of all the dinosaurs. Its name is *Compsognathus,* which means "graceful jaw."

What sort of life did this tiny beast live in a world full of giants? It probably trotted about on the muddy shores of shallow lakes in search of smaller reptiles and large insects to eat, for we can tell by the sharp little teeth in Compsognathus's fossil skull

that it was a meat eater. But it probably wasn't too fussy about the things it ate. If it chanced to come across a long-dead fish or shellfish that had been cast up on the shore, it gladly feasted on it.

The best fossil skeleton of Compsognathus was found in Bavaria, Germany, in stone that had once been lagoon mud. And there was a very lucky "extra" with this skeleton. Inside it, right where Compsognathus's stomach would have been, there was another skeleton of a very tiny creature. A careful examination of this showed it to be the skeleton of a little lizard that Compsognathus had swallowed whole. Thus, thanks to a bit of good luck, we know exactly one sort of thing Compsognathus ate. We also know that Compsognathus must have been a quick, skillful hunter, for it couldn't have been easy to catch a fast little lizard.

Most of the little animals that Compsognathus saw and hunted were much like animals that live today—lizards, turtles, and various kinds of insects. But as Compsognathus scurried about on the banks of its little lagoon world, it may have seen two other small creatures which, although they

Dapedius

32

Pterodactylus

COMPSOGNATHUS

were not dinosaurs, were not like any animal living today.

One was a flying reptile—like a lizard with wings! It is called Pterodactylus. Scientists think it probably lived among trees on the edge of lagoons where Compsognathus also lived.

Pterodactyluses were small, slim creatures, just about the size of a sparrow. Their wings were like thin flaps of leather attached to their arms and body. A Pterodactylus's jaws were long and pointed, like a bird's beak, and partly filled with sharp, wickedly curved little teeth. There were claws on its wings and feet, which probably helped it scramble up a tree trunk as easily as a squirrel does.

In many ways Pterodactylus was like a bird even though it wasn't at all related to birds. Its bones were hollow, as a bird's bones are, and it was probably warm-blooded, like birds and mammals. This means it was very active, not at all slow and sluggish as reptiles often are. On its flimsy wings it soared and glided over the lagoon, swooping down to snatch up tiny fish and perhaps snapping up insects in midair. Because of the way its wings were shaped, some scientists think it may have slept as bats do, hanging head down from a branch with its wings wrapped around itself.

Pterodactylus was one of a number of different kinds of flying reptiles that we call *pterosaurs*. Although these creatures were somewhat like birds, they had no feathers. For a time, scientists thought they might have been furry, like a cat or dog, but it is now known that this

Pterodactylus

was not so. The wings and body of Pterodactylus and other pterosaurs were probably covered with scaly skin like that of the reptiles of today.

The other creature that may have lived near the lagoon along with Compsognathus was also winged. But unlike Pterodactylus, this animal had feathers. It was a winged reptilelike creature with feathers—a strange sort of bird!

This odd creature is called *Archaeopteryx*. Archaeopteryx means "ancient wing," and it was truly a bird, according to scientists. The fossil skeletons of Archaeopteryx provide positive evidence that reptiles are the ancestors of birds, for Archaeopteryx had 17 feathers on each wing, and feathers on its legs, body, and tail. But its head was a little reptile head, and instead of a beak, it had jaws full of little needle-sharp teeth. Its tail, beneath the feathers, was a long, snaky reptile tail. And on each of the wings was a little clawed reptile hand. Like Pterodactylus, Archaeopteryx could climb trees.

Even though it had feathers, Archaeopteryx probably wasn't a very good flyer, perhaps not even as good a flyer as Pterodactylus. Its wings were too weak to have gotten it off the ground, so it must have flown by hopping out of high trees and spreading its wings to glide and soar. It probably didn't do much wing flapping.

This means that if Archaeopteryx had to alight on the ground for any reason, it must have been helpless until it could waddle to the nearest tree and climb to safety. There may have been times when an Archaeop-

Archaeopteryx

teryx was trapped on the ground and could not move fast enough to escape the sharp, little teeth of a Compsognathus that happened by. Archaeopteryx was no bigger than a pigeon, so Compsognathus could probably have easily overcome it.

It sounds as if Compsognathus was the undisputed king of its little world, living off smaller, more helpless creatures and having an easy time of it. But this may not have been the case, for even though Compsognathus was a flesh eater, its own small size made it fair game for bigger flesh eaters. Giant Allosaurus or Megalosaurus probably wouldn't have noticed such a tiny creature. But there were other flesh eaters that were only two or three times bigger than Compsognathus, and it would have been just the right size to make a hearty meal for one of them!

These other small flesh eaters were members of Compsognathus's own family, the

coelurosaurs. They were fast-moving reptiles, about 6 feet long and 3 feet high, with slender, fingerlike claws they probably used for grabbing up quick, little creatures that skittered over the ground. One of these coelurosaurs that lived in North America has been named *Ornitholestes,* which means "bird catcher," because some scientists think it may have been quick enough to leap up and grab birds out of the air if they swooped too low. But this is most doubtful.

Despite their small size, these flesh-eating coelurosaurs were widespread and successful dinosaurs. Their fossil bones have been found in North and South America, Asia, Africa, and Australia, and little three-toed footprints made by some of them have been found in England.

And some of them lived in continental Europe where, from time to time, they may have dined on their cousin Compsognathus, the smallest of them all.

Unfolding Ferns

Ornitholestes

Anatosaurus — THE DUCK-BILLED DINOSAUR

IF YOU could have stood on the shore of almost any North American lagoon about 80 million years ago, sooner or later you might have seen what seemed to be a huge duck swimming toward you. But as it neared the shore and stood up to wade out of the water on its two hind legs, you would have seen that it was a dinosaur— a dinosaur with a long, narrow head and jaws shaped remarkably like the bill of a duck or goose.

Scientists call this odd creature *Anatosaurus,* which means "goose lizard." But it's more commonly called a duck-billed dinosaur. Eighty million years ago duck-billed dinosaurs, or hadrosaurs, were one of the most common kinds of dinosaurs in North America.

Although duck-billed dinosaurs such as Anatosaurus seem built for swimming, with webbed feet and flat, oarlike tails, they were not water-dwelling reptiles like crocodiles or alligators. They probably spent a great deal more time on land than in water, for it is known that they ate such things as pine needles, twigs, fruit, and seeds, which are mostly found in forests. Anatosaurus probably walked about on its two back legs to browse on twigs and leaves, and got down on all fours to search for low-growing shoots and fallen seeds and fruit.

Anatosauruses and other kinds of hadrosaurs probably lived in herds, and there is evidence that the adults looked after the young ones. Apparently, as a herd moved about from place to place, the young hadrosaurs were kept in the middle of the group, surrounded by full-grown adults that could protect them. While hadrosaurs had no claws or sharp teeth with which to defend themselves, they had powerful tails that they may have used as weapons. A full-grown Anatosaurus was about 33 feet long. A whiplike slap of its big tail could have knocked even a big Tyrannosaurus off its feet. On the other hand, perhaps a hadrosaur's best defense was to simply run away. They apparently had good eyesight, hearing, and a keen sense of smell, and could have seen, heard, or smelled an approaching flesh eater in plenty of time to flee.

Hadrosaurs were apparently very good parents. Fossil nests, eggs, and baby skeletons of one kind of hadrosaur have been found, showing that mother hadrosaurs cared for their young much as many kinds of birds do. A mother pushed mud together to form a mound, scooped a shallow pit in

ANATOSAURUS

Turtle   Lungfish

Present-day Gila Monster

the top, and laid her eggs in the pit. She crouched over the eggs to keep them warm and help them hatch. When they hatched, the mother went off to bring back mouthfuls of food to drop in the nest for the babies to eat. Even while she was away, the babies were protected, because a great many nests were always built close together, and there were always some mothers around to keep an eye on things.

We know a good deal more about what a live Anatosaurus looked like than we do about the appearance of most other dinosaurs, thanks to two wonderful mummylike fossils of these animals that were found in Wyoming many years ago. These stone "mummies" show things that plain fossil bones could never reveal. When the animals died, their skin, instead of rotting away, dried up and became tightly stretched across the bones of their skeletons, like the skin of a mummy. Both the skin and skeletons turned to stone. And so these fossils show us that Anatosaurus had webbed front feet and a sort of ruffle of skin that ran down its back to the end of the tail, and they show us what its skin was like.

The skin of Anatosaurus was thick and leathery and covered all over with tiny bumps mixed with little clusters of bigger bumps. Anatosaurus's skin was apparently very much like the skin of the little lizard called a Gila monster, which lives today in the same part of western North America where Anatosaurus lived those millions of years ago.

One of the "mummies" tells us something about the place where Anatosaurus lived and gives us a dramatic picture of how this dinosaur died. The hadrosaur's body was stretched out full length with one leg reaching down and with its bill pointing straight up. The unfortunate animal had wandered into a patch of quicksand or into a deep, muddy bog and sank to its death, vainly trying to keep its head above the mud so it could breathe.

Anatosaurus was one of the last kinds of hadrosaurs. Several other kinds lived when it did, and some lived much earlier. Kritosaurus, Corythosaurus, and Lambeosaurus were three duckbills that lived millions of years before Anatosaurus, but they were all its relatives. Their bodies were shaped almost exactly like Anatosaurus's body, but their heads were quite different. Kritosaurus had a big bump on its nose that made its jaws look more like a parrot's beak than a duck's bill. Corythosaurus had a bony crest shaped like a half circle on its head. And on Lambeosaurus's head was a crest shaped like a hatchet!

Oddest of all when it came to fancy head decorations was Parasaurolophus, a duck-billed dinosaur that lived at about the same time as Anatosaurus. Parasaurolophus had a long, curved tube of bone that stuck far out of the back of its head.

Why did these duck-billed dinosaurs have such odd bumps and bony decorations on their heads? Was there a reason for them, or were they just for show? Most scientists think there was a reason, and there are several theories as to what it might have been.

One idea is that these head decorations

Corythosaurus

Lambeosaurus

could have been a means of identification. The first thing a newly hatched hadrosaur saw was its mother, and it would quickly become familiar with the appearance of her crest. From then on it would know that all such creatures with that sort of crest were its own kind, and it wouldn't try to attach itself to some other kind of hadrosaur by mistake.

Another idea is that the head decorations might have helped give a hadrosaur an extra-special sense of smell. All the bony crests were hollow, and tubes ran from the crests through the duckbill's skull to its nose, so that when the duckbill took a breath, the air went up into its crest. Perhaps this enabled the animal to hold onto a scent longer, which could have helped warn it sooner of an approaching flesh eater.

And maybe these crests were noisemakers. Maybe they were like trumpets, so that sounds the duckbills made echoed and sounded louder. Just imagine what hootings and bellowings these big animals might have made!

Anatosaurus didn't have a fancy ornament on its head as most of its relatives did. In fact, Anatosaurus is sometimes called a "flat-headed" duckbill. But there was one special feature that Anatosaurus shared with all other duckbills. Teeth! All these dinosaurs had hundreds of teeth that formed a rough sort of solid pavement on their upper and lower jaws, back behind the bill!

Duckbills needed lots of teeth because of the way they ate. They ground tough twigs to a pulp by rubbing them between their upper and lower teeth. All this grinding slowly wore the teeth down. By examining Anatosaurus skulls, scientists have found that a duckbill was always growing new teeth that pushed up to replace those that wore out. A duckbill such as Anatosaurus regularly used more than 2,000 teeth during its lifetime!

Parasaurolophus

Protoceratops — THE EGG LAYER

OUR KNOWLEDGE of dinosaurs is like a picture puzzle with a lot of missing pieces. Each missing piece is an unanswered question. But every once in a while a great discovery is made that lets us put a new piece into the puzzle.

In 1922 a group of American scientists in the Gobi desert of Mongolia found the fossil skull of a new kind of dinosaur. Its mouth was a hard, horny beak, like the beak of a parrot. Such a mouth was well designed for snipping off the tops of low-growing plants. Out of the back of the skull grew a curved, bony shield that must have spread back over the animal's neck. Scientists looked at this bony shield and the beaked jaws and named the new dinosaur Protoceratops.

Now *Protoceratops* means "first horned face." Why was such a name given to an animal that had no horns? Why wasn't this dinosaur called by a name that meant "shield head" or perhaps "parrot beak?" Actually, there was a good reason for scientists to name the animal as they did. They realized that this dinosaur was related to some other dinosaurs they had known about for a long time, a whole family of dinosaurs that had beaked mouths, bony shields growing out of their heads, and *horns*. These dinosaurs had been named *ceratopsians*, which means "horned faces." And Protoceratops was named *"first horned face"* because the scientists felt that Protoceratops probably looked very much like the first kinds of ceratopsian dinosaurs.

Finding a new dinosaur that belonged to a family of well-known dinosaurs was a great discovery that put an important piece into the picture puzzle of dinosaur knowledge. But even more was to come.

A year after the Protoceratops skull had been found, a small group of men—the same scientists who had found the skull—stood beside a sandstone cliff in the hot, parched Gobi desert. They were clustered around one man who held something in his hands—a creamy white object about the size and shape of a baked potato.

"Gentlemen," said the man, turning the thing over in his hands, "there is no doubt about it. You are looking at the first dinosaur egg ever found!"

These men had made one of the greatest discoveries in all the history of fossil hunting. For many years one of the biggest questions in the minds of most people who studied dinosaurs was, How were baby

PROTOCERATOPS

Another Kind of Ceratopsian (Styracosaurus)

dinosaurs born? Since dinosaurs were reptiles, and most reptiles hatch from eggs, it was generally believed that dinosaur babies probably hatched from eggs, too. But there was no way to be sure of this, and it seemed as if there never would be—for it was hardly possible that such a fragile thing as an egg could leave any kind of trace after millions of years.

But now eggs had been found. There were about 20 of them, whole and in pieces, in a chunk of weathered red sandstone. This showed that dinosaurs not only laid eggs but laid them in nests, just as many modern reptiles do. And the scientists were even fairly sure they knew what kind of dinosaur had laid these eggs. It seemed to be none other than the dinosaur they had recently discovered—Protoceratops!

About 100 million years ago the Gobi desert was a flat, sandy plain dotted with small, scrubby plants. The mother Protoceratops hunted for a place to lay her eggs. She was a short, squat reptile, only about 6 feet long from the end of her tail to her beaked nose. Moving slowly along the edge of a small pond, she examined one sand dune after another. She wanted a place where the sand was neither too coarse nor too fine.

At last she found a dune that suited her. With her clawed, five-toed front feet, she scooped out a broad, shallow pit. Crouching over this, she began to lay her eggs.

One by one the eggs plopped into the pit until, after a time, about 20 of them lay clustered in three layers at the bottom. They looked like small, white baked potatoes. Their shells were leathery and covered with tiny wrinkles.

Kicking with her back legs, the mother Protoceratops shoveled sand into the pit until the eggs were loosely covered. Then she shuffled off toward a distant clump of plants from which she began to clip bunches of leaves.

Although the mother Protoceratops left it all up to the warmth of the sun to hatch the eggs, she very probably stayed nearby to keep an eye on them as they were hatching. In fact, she was probably part of a small herd that would have all helped guard the eggs, for there were surely other dinosaurs in the area that would have dug up the eggs and eaten them, given the chance. Although a Protoceratops had no sharp teeth or claws, its sharp-edged beak would have made a good defensive weapon. So, guarded by the adults, the eggs would lie beneath the sun-heated sand until the baby dinosaurs inside them would break through the shells and push up through the sand into the world.

But these Protoceratops babies were never to know life. Across the desert a brisk wind began to blow. The air became filled with whirling particles of sand. The wind increased in power until the whole great plain resounded with its wailing shriek. Savagely the wind lifted up tons of loose sand and flung them through the air in a yellow cloud.

For hours the sandstorm raged. And when the wind finally sank to a whisper and then died away, the Protoceratops eggs were buried deep under several feet of sand. With no air able to reach through this thick blanket, the unborn babies died inside their eggs.

As the insides of the eggs began to dry up, the weight of the sand cracked the shells. Through those cracks sand trickled into the eggs, tightly filling the shells. Now the *shapes* of the eggs were preserved— they couldn't be mashed flat.

Years passed, then whole centuries. More sand, carried by years of blowing winds, piled atop the eggs and buried them ever deeper. Minerals, carried by trickles of water from infrequent rains, soaked slowly through the close-packed sand and reached the eggs. These minerals seeped through the cracks in the shells and reached the tiny bones of the unhatched baby dinosaurs. And very, very slowly, each microscopic bit of eggshell or bone was replaced by mineral that hardened into rock. In this way the eggs became perfect petrified copies of themselves—stone fossils that were the exact size and shape of the originals.

Centuries went by. Thousands of years went by. Millions of years went by. The red desert sand hardened into sandstone, encasing the eggs in solid rock.

More millions of years passed. Each day the wind blew, the sun burned down. Occasional rains lashed the soft rock. Slowly the sandstone wore away into cliffs and gullies. And, by chance, the eggs that had been deeply buried became exposed in the side of a cliff, awaiting discovery by that little group of scientists.

That discovery was only a beginning. The scientists found more than 70 eggs, together with complete skeletons of newly hatched, half-grown, and adult protoceratopsians. They even found skeletons of unhatched babies in some of the eggs that had broken open. It was one of the greatest fossil finds ever made—a life history of a dinosaur from egg to adult!

Other dinosaur eggs have since been found. But little Protoceratops will always be famous as the dinosaur that first showed us how dinosaur babies were born. That discovery put one of the biggest and most important pieces into our picture puzzle of dinosaur knowledge.

Pteranodon

Tyrannosaurus

Hesperornis

Triceratops—THE THREE-HORNED FACE

SEVENTY MILLION years ago, the western part of North America was about as warm and moist as Florida is today. There were great swamps and forests of palm trees mixed with ginkgoes, figs, and giant redwoods. And on the edges of the forests where there were vast plains, herds of four-footed dinosaurs browsed on the spiky fronds of palm trees and cycads.

They were fairly large dinosaurs, up to about 30 feet long and 10 feet high—much longer than a big elephant but not quite as tall. Their tails were short and heavy, and their legs were thick, with broad, flat feet to support the weight of their bodies. Their toes were clawed—three claws on the toes of their front feet and four on the back— but the claws were small and blunt, like little hooves.

These dinosaurs had enormous heads that were nearly a third as long as their whole bodies. And out of the backs of their heads grew big shields of bone that spread out to cover their necks and shoulders. Their jaws were curved like parrotbeaks and they browsed by cocking their heads to one side and snipping off leaves and fronds with their beaked mouths, as neatly as you might snip flower stems with a scissors.

But the most striking thing about these bulky reptiles were the horns that stuck up from their heads—a sharp, 3-foot-long horn above each eye, and a short, thick horn that poked up from the nose. It is from these horns that this dinosaur gets the name *Triceratops,* which means "three-horned face."

Even though Triceratops was a harmless plant eater, those horns on its head weren't just for show. Triceratops used them. It was a fighter! We know this because scars and scratches that were made by the horns of other triceratopsians have been found on the bony shields of fossil Triceratops skulls. Male horned dinosaurs may have fought each other at times, just as deer, antelope, and other horned animals fight each other today. What a fearsome sight it must have been when two of these massive, 10-ton beasts charged headlong at each other, with the earth shivering beneath their thudding feet. They may have nipped at each other with their parrotbeaks as they dodged and sidestepped, jerking and twisting their big heads to jab and stab with their horns. Sometimes, apparently, they fought so viciously that one animal's horn would break against another's bony

Pteranodon

27'

shield, for a Triceratops skull has been found with a broken horn that had healed and was shorter than the horn on the other side of the face.

Since we know for sure that Triceratops fought others of its own kind, we can be sure it would have fought just as savagely to defend itself from any flesh eater that attacked it. Such fights might have happened, for Triceratops lived at the same time and in the same place as the giant flesh eater Tyrannosaurus. If Tyrannosauruses were active hunters, and not just scavengers, they may have often prowled near Triceratops herds, watching for a chance to pounce on a young horned-face that strayed too far from the others. But sooner or later, a prowling Tyrannosaurus might have been challenged by one or more members of the herd. We can use our imagination to picture what could have happened then. . . .

The Tyrannosaurus crouches motionless some distance from the mass of browsing horned faces. Those on the edge of the herd, nearest to the flesh eater, glance toward it warily from time to time.

Then abruptly, a large male Triceratops lowers its head, and with horns pointing forward, launches itself at Tyrannosaurus like a modern army tank charging full speed at an enemy! The tyrannosaur moves aside as the horned dinosaur thunders past, but a horn grazes the flesh eater's leg.

The Triceratops slows to a stop and quickly turns to face its foe. The Tyrannosaurus paces swiftly around the three-horned face, seeking to catch the plant eater off guard so it can leap upon its back, but the Tricera-

tops wheels its body around, keeping its fierce horns always pointed at the enemy.

Once again the Triceratops hurls itself suddenly forward, and this time the Tyrannosaurus isn't quick enough. The horned dinosaur slams into the flesh eater, jerking its head upward savagely so that its two long horns rip deep into the tyrannosaur's belly! The impact lifts the flesh eater off its feet and hurls it backward to sprawl on the ground. Moving forward quickly, the Triceratops jabs its horn again and again into the fallen tyrannosaur's body.

If such fights did occur, a Tyrannosaurus probably won more often than not.

There were a number of different kinds, or species, of Triceratops. They were all just about the same except for slight differences in size, shape of horns, and so on. Each species probably formed a large herd, or herds, of its own.

Triceratops was one of the last and biggest of the horned dinosaurs. It had a close relative, Torosaurus, that lived at about the same time and looked much like Triceratops except that its bony head shield was longer and wider, spreading halfway over Torosaurus's back. Both these beasts came from a big family of horned dinosaurs that lived in North America for several million years.

Pentaceratops, which lived a few million years earlier than Triceratops and Torosaurus, looked much like them except that it was slightly smaller. Also, in addition to the three horns on the top of its head, it had a sort of horn on each side of its lower jaw. *Pentaceratops* means "five-horned face."

46

Another horned dinosaur called Monoclonius lived still earlier by a few million years. It had two small horns above its eyes and one very long horn on its nose, just the opposite of Triceratops. Styracosaurus also had a long horn on its nose. It had no horns at all above its eyes, but sticking up from the edges of its bony shield were six long, wickedly pointed spikes. Chasmosaurus, still another early horned dinosaur, had two short horns above its eyes and a single short horn on its nose.

There was also one kind of horned-face that had no horns. Instead, *Pachyrhinosaurus* ("thick-nosed lizard") had a broad, thick patch of bone covering its forehead. Males probably used these bony patches to fight with at mating time, bumping their heads together as goats of today do.

While Triceratops's head shield was solid bone, the shields of all these other horned dinosaurs had large holes in them, which were covered over with tough skin. This made the shields much lighter, which was important because a horned-face such as Torosaurus would hardly have been able to move its head if its huge shield had been solid. However, shields with holes in them wouldn't have been of much use for defense, so scientists think dinosaurs that had such shields must have used them differently than Triceratops did. Perhaps they were used to frighten would-be attackers. When a Torosaurus lowered its head, its huge shield would have lifted straight up, making the Torosaurus suddenly look much bigger to anything facing it head-on. This could have startled an attacker into fleeing.

Most kinds of dinosaurs that lived in America also lived in many other parts of the world. But nearly all the fossils of horned dinosaurs have been found only in the western part of North America. A few have been found in Asia, but none anywhere else. Apparently in that far-off time, there were natural barriers of some kind that kept the horned dinosaurs from spreading into the eastern part of North America or into Europe and Africa.

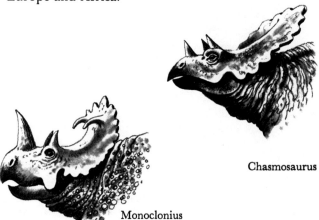

Chasmosaurus

Monoclonius

Tyrannosaurus — KILLER OR SCAVENGER?

JUST STANDING in front of the fossil skeleton of the dinosaur called Tyrannosaurus rex is enough to give you the shivers, because it's easy to imagine what this monster looked like when it was alive. It was a creature out of a nightmare—the biggest, most powerful flesh-eating animal that has ever walked the earth and perhaps the most terrible killer as well!

Tyrannosaurus walked on its two strong, heavy back legs, and when standing upright, was about 20 feet high. A tall man would have reached only to its knee. Its powerful body was nearly 40 feet long and weighed about 7½ tons—longer than a railroad boxcar and about equal to the biggest kind of elephant. The claws on Tyrannosaurus's three-toed feet were about 8 inches long. Its huge head was nearly 5 feet long and its jaws were filled with inch-thick, 6-inch-long teeth, pointed like daggers and saw-toothed like the cutting edge of a steak knife.

Tyrannosaurus rex means "king tyrant lizard." A tyrant is a cruel and powerful ruler who has the power of life and death over his subjects. And Tyrannosaurus certainly seems to fit that description. Some scientists think it was the king of beasts in its ancient world, and that almost any other dinosaur that crossed its path was marked for attack from those dagger-sharp teeth and terrible tearing claws. It may have been the most savage hunter that ever walked on land.

However, other scientists are not so sure about this. They don't think that Tyrannosaurus was a hunter at all. They think it was merely a big scavenger, like a vulture or jackal—the kind of animal that seldom if ever kills anything for itself, but instead eats the bodies of any dead animals it happens to find.

The tyrant reptile king lived about 70 million years ago in the western part of North America. It was the biggest of all the flesh-eating dinosaurs in the world, but it wasn't the only one of its time. It had a sort of cousin called Albertosaurus (because its fossil bones were found in Alberta, Canada) that lived at about the same time and in the same part of the country as Tyrannosaurus. Albertosaurus looked much like Tyrannosaurus but was considerably smaller. And there was a very strange flesh-eating dinosaur named Spinosaurus that lived where Egypt is today. This creature, too, looked much like Tyrannosaurus, but on its back

Tyrannosaurus

Comparative Size of a Six-foot Man

48

TYRANNOSAURUS

Anatosaurus

was a huge fin as much as 6 feet high, shaped like the fin on the back of a sailfish. Most scientists think this fin may have helped keep Spinosaurus from getting too hot or too cool.

The North American Tyrannosaurus wasn't the only Tyrannosaurus in the world. A slightly different kind of Tyrannosaurus also lived in China.

The countryside through which Tyrannosaurus roamed was the home of vast numbers of duck-billed dinosaurs and horned dinosaurs as well as armored dinosaurs and several other kinds of creatures. Some of these would have been easier prey than others. The armored dinosaurs were well-protected and hard to overcome. The horned dinosaurs lived in big herds and were well able to defend themselves. If Tyrannosauruses were hunters, the creatures they probably hunted most often were the duckbills. Let us take an imaginary trip back through time and see how a Tyrannosaurus might have done its hunting.

The huge flesh eater strides along with its head and body bent forward and its tail stretched straight out. It rather resembles a stalking bird in search of a worm.

The longer the Tyrannosaurus hunts, the greater its hunger grows. Rounding a clump of redwood trees, it comes suddenly upon an armored ankylosaur. The armored dinosaur is much too slow to run, so it depends on its armor to save it. Quickly it squats down, tucking its legs under itself.

The Tyrannosaurus bends low and snaps at the ankylosaur's armored back. Its teeth make a rasping sound against the hard, bony armor. The Tyrannosaurus claws at the ankylosaur with one of its big, taloned feet. But the armored dinosaur's broad, flat body hugs the ground like a boulder, and Tyrannosaurus's claws barely scratch the armor.

The Tyrannosaurus is ravenously hungry now, and it becomes enraged. It bites again at the ankylosaur's back. Then suddenly, from among the trees where a broad river winds through the plain, there is a sound of splashing and snorting. The Tyrannosaurus's head jerks up and it glares toward the river. The flesh eater knows those sounds. There is prey near the river that will be easier to overcome than the ankylosaur!

Leaving the armored dinosaur still crouched in its tracks, the Tyrannosaurus lopes toward the sounds. On the riverbank three duck-billed Anatosauruses, dripping from their swim across the river, are browsing on the needles of pine trees growing near the river. Suddenly, the Tyrannosaurus bursts through the trees and is upon them!

The duckbills scatter as quickly as they can, scrambling desperately toward the water in which they will be safe. But one duckbill is too late and too slow. In three strides the Tyrannosaurus has caught up with it. The flesh eater's enormous mouth gapes wider for an instant, then the fierce teeth crunch into the back of the duckbill's neck. The weight of the Tyrannosaurus's body crushes the duckbill to the ground. With a savage wrench of its jaws, the flesh eater nearly severs the duckbill's head from its body.

Now the Tyrannosaurus crouches so that its huge body is nearly lying across that of the dead anatosaur. It sinks its teeth into its prey and with another single twist of its neck rips away an enormous chunk of flesh. Swallowing this in a gulp, it buries its jaws once more in the duckbill's flesh, hardly waiting to swallow one gob of meat before it is gouging out another.

Half an hour later, the Tyrannosaurus's great appetite is satisfied. It rises slowly, using its tiny but strong arms to push itself up. Moving lazily, it passes out of sight among the trees.

Many scientists think that's how Tyrannosaurus got its food—savagely hunting and killing its prey. But the scientists who think that Tyrannosaurus was a scavenger point out that because of the way Tyran-

nosaurus's hip bones were formed, it probably couldn't do more than just waddle along slowly, and most other dinosaurs would have been able to outrun it. And a careful examination of some Tyrannosaurus teeth seemed to show that they weren't strong enough for fighting, but could only have been used for eating soft, perhaps slightly rotten, meat. So these scientists are sure that Tyrannosaurus generally just waddled about in search of dead creatures to eat and never did any hunting or fighting.

But that seems hard to believe. For when we look at the fossil skeleton of this great beast—the enormous head with its sharp, bristling teeth and the powerful body—it's hard not to think of Tyrannosaurus as a terrible killer, truly the king of beasts not only for its own time but for all time to come.

51

Ankylosaurus — THE ARMORED DINOSAUR

ANKYLOSAURUS was a dinosaur that wore armor and carried a club!

Ankylosaurus means "stiff lizard," but a better name for this creature might have been "bumpy lizard"! For Ankylosaurus's head, neck, back, and tail were covered with a bumpy armor of thick, rock-hard ovals of bone embedded in tough skin. This armor was not stiff and solid like the shell of a turtle; it was flexible, like the bony shell of a modern armadillo.

But Ankylosaurus undoubtedly used its armor in the same way that a turtle does. If Ankylosaurus was attacked, all it had to do was crouch down with its legs tucked beneath itself and its soft throat and belly pressed tightly against the ground. In this position there was nothing for an attacker to bite but a mass of bony bumps. And the hungry Tyrannosaurus or other flesh eater that tried to bite through an Ankylosaurus's armor would have found itself with a mouth full of broken teeth.

However, Ankylosaurus didn't depend on its armor alone for protection. It could fight, and fight well. Its teeth were blunt and weak, and it had no sharp claws, but its tail was thick and powerful and tipped with a huge, round mass of bone—nothing less than a massive and deadly club! When Ankylosaurus was attacked it probably waited until its tail was in striking distance of the attacker, and then—THUMP! The tail whipped around and smashed into the other dinosaur's legs or body with enough force to crack bones and send it sprawling. And the flesh eater whose leg was broken by a blow from an ankylosaur's tail was as good as dead, for it would be unable to walk and hunt and would starve to death.

Ankylosaurus was a fair-sized dinosaur, from 15 to 20 feet long and 6 feet high at the hips. It was built as solidly as a boulder, with a wide, bulky body and squat, solid legs like the legs of an elephant. Its feet, too, were broad and flat like an elephant's feet, and for the same reason—they had to support the weight of a heavy body.

Ankylosaurus's head was broad and blunt and looked much like the head of a horned lizard of today. This resemblance was increased by shelves of bone that stuck out above its eyes, coming to points on each side of its head. These shelves helped protect Ankylosaurus's eyes. Even its eyelids had bony shields embedded in them!

It's easy to imagine this broad, bulky

Tyrannosaurus

ANKYLOSAURUS

52

beast crunching through the underbrush like a big armored tank, its head swinging from side to side as it peered about with its little eyes for the kind of soft plants its weak teeth could chew. Despite its bulk and armor and terrible tail, Ankylosaurus was really a harmless reptile that spent most of its time looking for food and would only fight if attacked.

There were many different kinds of these bone-armored, plant-eating dinosaurs living in all parts of the world from about 130 million to 70 million years ago. Some lived at the same time as Ankylosaurus, and some lived millions of years earlier. They all belonged to the ankylosaur family, but they all have different names. And each had its own kind of armor, and usually, its own special kind of weapon on its tail.

Paleoscincus, which means "ancient lizard," lived in North America about 80 million years ago, some 10 million years before Ankylosaurus. The two animals looked much alike and were about the same size, but Paleoscincus's armor consisted of bands of bony rectangles running down its back and tail, and rows of big, sharp spikes along its sides. Paleoscincus must have depended mostly on its armor for protection, because it doesn't seem to have had a club on its tail.

Another North American armored dinosaur was *Nodosaurus,* meaning "knobbed lizard." Its 12-foot-long body was covered· with round bumps of bone. Nodosaurus was related to Paleoscincus, and like that animal, did not have a club tail either. Its tail was like a long, stiff rod of bone. It

probably couldn't have used such a tail as a weapon and depended entirely on its armor for protection.

Euoplocephalus was another North American ankylosaur. In fact, it was the ancestor of Ankylosaurus. It was only about half as long as Ankylosaurus, and its armor consisted of big, pointed knobs that stuck up all over its body. On the end of its tail was a huge ball of bone with sharp ridges on it.

Pinacosaurus was an armored dinosaur that lived in Mongolia and was related to Ankylosaurus and Euoplocephalus. Sharp spikes pointed up from its back, sides, legs, and tail. Its tail was quite a bit longer than the tails of most other armored dinosaurs and ended in a broad, flat piece of bone with sharp edges. It looked like a battle-ax, and that's probably what Pinacosaurus used it for!

Polacanthus and Acanthopholis were two kinds of armored dinosaurs that lived in what is now England and northern Europe. They were both somewhat smaller than Ankylosaurus, and their bodies were much slimmer, with longer legs, necks, and tails. Polacanthus had a double row of enormous, sharp horns running up its back to its hips. A big, curved shield of bone covered its hips, and then a double row of flat, bony points ran all the way down to the end of its tail. Acanthopholis had a whole mixture of spikes, knobs, bumps, and rectangles covering its body.

And there were other members of the ankylosaur family besides these. Fossils of nearly 30 different kinds of these bulky, armored beasts have been found in North and South America, Europe, and Asia. It is believed that these heavy, bulky reptiles probably lived on dry upland plains where the ground was hard enough to support their weight.

Almost all the Ankylosaur remains that have been found were upside down. It was once believed that these might have been the remains of Ankylosaurs that had been turned over and killed by flesh eaters, but most scientists now think it would have been almost impossible for even a big Tyrannosaurus to overturn as bulky and heavy a beast as an adult Ankylosaurus. More likely, these were the remains of Ankylosaurs that might have been caught in flash floods and their bodies washed down into rivers, where they turned over from the weight of the armor on the back, and sank to the bottom. It is possible, however, that a small, young, not too heavy Ankylosaur might have been turned over by a big, persistent Tyrannosaur using its powerful legs and clawed feet. Once on its back the Ankylosaur would have been as helpless as an overturned turtle, and the flesh eater could have begun tearing into its unprotected throat and belly.

Armored dinosaurs undoubtedly did become food for hungry flesh eaters from time to time, but this certainly must not have happened very often. For the most part these squat, bulky creatures must have been quite safe inside their thick shells of bony armor and well defended by their war-club tails. Ankylosaurs seem to have been quite common in prehistoric times; there were many different kinds of them, and they were around for nearly 60 million years. This seems to prove that the combination of armor and a war-club tail was pretty successful.

Struthiomimus — THE OSTRICH DINOSAUR

THE MIDDAY SUN gleams hotly on the gray-green surface of a broad, winding river. Above the water dragonflies dart and hover in search of prey. On the muddy banks a variety of creatures—frogs, turtles, snakes, and a host of insects—creep, crawl, hop, and stalk in search of food.

Moving along the riverbank is an odd, ungainly creature. It has a tiny head perched atop a long, thin neck. It strides along on two birdlike back legs, holding its smaller front legs against its chest, kangaroo fashion. A long, slender tail stretches stiffly out behind it, and its head bobs with every step it takes.

Abruptly the creature stops. It turns its head jerkily from side to side, surveying the stretch of riverbank and the nearby forest edge for a sign of danger. Satisfied that all is well, it cocks its head and peers at the ground by its feet where something has caught its attention.

Bending down, it scrabbles in the earth with its three-fingered hands. After a few moments it straightens up, holding an egg, about the size and shape of a potato, that it has dug out of the muddy earth. Curving its neck, the animal prods fiercely at the egg with its beaklike jaws. Its efforts to break the shell are shortly rewarded, and it slurps down the egg's contents.

Dropping the empty shell, the creature cocks its head and peers again at the ground. It stoops once more, as if to resume digging. But suddenly its body whips upright. It stands frozen, with head half-turned and eyes staring unblinkingly toward the forest, some distance away.

From among the trees another creature appears. It is a much larger animal, with a heavy body and tail and powerful legs. Its massive head is split into huge jaws filled with sharp teeth. The jaws widen as it catches sight of the long-necked creature. With immense strides it moves forward.

But fast as a finger snap, the long-necked creature is running away. It moves with surprising speed, its skinny legs kicking up spurts of dirt as they churn up and down. It is soon no more than a dot in the distance, safely out of reach . . . .

That imaginary look into the past illustrates what was probably a typical adventure in the life of a most curious dinosaur that lived on the North American continent about 75 million years ago. It is called *Struthiomimus*, which means "ostrich imitator." And this gawky reptile of

Crocodiles

STRUTHIOMIMUS

Frogs   Pachyophis

long ago certainly was a remarkable "imitation" of that big, gawky bird, the ostrich, which lives today in the deserts of Africa.

Of course, no one ever saw a live Struthiomimus, but its fossil skeleton looks very much like the skeleton of a modern ostrich. They are both about the same size—8 feet tall. Both have the same kind of legs. Both have ridiculously tiny heads on top of identically long, skinny necks. And most unusual for a dinosaur, Struthiomimus had no teeth. It had a toothless bill that was almost exactly like the bill of an ostrich!

There were differences between the two creatures, of course, for Struthiomimus was a reptile and an ostrich is a bird. Struthiomimus had long, slender arms—very much like human arms—instead of wings, and a dry, leathery skin instead of feathers. And it had a long reptilian tail.

But because Struthiomimus was generally so much like an ostrich, most scientists think it probably acted much as an ostrich does. For example, we know that an ostrich can run faster than a racehorse, and since Struthiomimus had the same kind of legs, it was undoubtedly a mighty fast runner, too. Running was probably its way of protecting itself, for while an ostrich can kick hard enough to break a lion's back, and Struthiomimus's legs were equally powerful, kicking would have done the dinosaur no good. Its chief danger was from the monster, flesh-eating Tyrannosaurus and the smaller, but equally terrible Albertosaurus. Either of these creatures could have gobbled up a Struthiomimus as easily as you can eat a hot dog, and a kick wouldn't

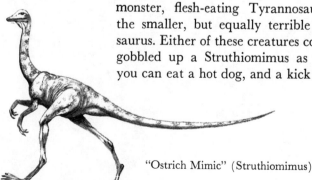

Ostrich

"Ostrich Mimic" (Struthiomimus)

have bothered them any more than a mosquito bite.

Even though it had no teeth, Struthiomimus was probably a meat eater. Its "pecking" beak was well equipped for snapping up insects, worms, and perhaps small, soft-bodied lizards, which it gulped down whole just as ostriches do today. Possibly it could have managed to eat some of the small, ratlike mammals that lived at that time, too.

Ostriches eat plants, and some scientists think that Struthiomimus may have eaten plants, too. With its handlike claws it would have been able to pull down the lower branches of trees so that it could nip off the soft leaves, buds, and fruit. However, other scientists doubt that Struthiomimus's bill was strong enough to chop up plant material.

Although ostriches don't eat eggs, most scientists think that Struthiomimus may have done so. With the whole world full of egg-laying reptiles there were undoubtedly plenty of eggs to be found, and Struthiomimus was well able to dig eggs out of nests and hold them in its hands while it cracked them with its beaklike jaws. For that matter, there were many kinds of birds in the world when Struthiomimus was alive, so it may have occasionally feasted on some of their eggs, too.

Struthiomimus wasn't the only kind of ostrich dinosaur. It had a cousin named *Ornithomimus*, which means "bird imitator" and which looked very much like Struthiomimus. Ornithomimus lived in North America, too, but fossils of both it

58

and Struthiomimus have also been found in Asia.

These ostrich dinosaurs were a widespread and successful group of dinosaurs. Most scientists think they should have been able to survive, perhaps right into modern times. But between 70 and 65 million years ago, Struthiomimus and all its kin became extinct just as mysteriously as did all the other dinosaurs.

There are a great many questions about dinosaurs, but the biggest question of all is, Why did they become extinct? Many other kinds of animals that lived at the time of the last dinosaurs are still in the world today—snakes, lizards, crocodiles, turtles, and many kinds of insects, fish, and sea animals. But every single kind of dinosaur is gone—big ones, small ones, plant eaters, and flesh eaters. And many other kinds of animals that lived at the time of the dinosaurs became extinct at about the same time. It was as if something came along and wiped out certain kinds of animals while leaving others unharmed. What could have done such a thing?

Many scientists think there is clear evidence that a terrible catastrophe ended the time of the dinosaurs. Apparently, a huge comet or meteorite collided with Earth. This caused a raging fire storm that swept many parts of the land. The collision also hurled many thousands of tons of dust into the sky. The smoke and dust encircled the world, so thick that little sunlight could get through for several months. Scientists think this caused much of the plant life to die and turned the weather cold. Plant-eating dinosaurs must have died out, and the meat eaters that lived off them soon followed.

Ornithomimus

Other scientists don't think it happened that way. They agree there is evidence of a terrible collision, but they don't think that's what killed off the dinosaurs. They point out that if the catastrophe had been bad enough to wipe out the dinosaurs, it should also have wiped out crocodiles, birds, and other creatures—which did not happen. They feel there is evidence that the dinosaurs were already dying off, for some reason, before the collision, and that they continued to die off, slowly, long after it. So scientists do not agree on what made the dinosaurs become extinct. No one knows for sure.

Phobosuchus

59

Mammals—THE FURRY BEASTS

SEVENTY MILLION years ago, a giant animal prowled through a hot, moist forest. From the tip of its long tail to its huge snout, it was nearly 50 feet in length, and its great head was nearly 20 feet above the ground. A tall man would have reached only to its knees. As the animal moved through the greenery, shafts of sunlight, slanting through the leaves, shimmered on the scales that covered the enormous body. For the creature was a reptile—a scaly-skinned reptile of the kind that have been named *dinosaurs*.

The world this dinosaur lived in was lit-erally a world of reptiles. Scores of different kinds of dinosaurs stalked and scampered and lumbered upon the land. In the seas were giant reptiles that resembled fish and legendary sea serpents. And in the air there were reptiles that flapped and soared on leathery wings. Reptiles were the "rulers" of the earth.

But as the giant dinosaur strode past a clump of ferns, a pair of bright little eyes gleamed out at it. An animal was hidden among the ferns—an animal that was com-pletely different from the dinosaur and every other reptile. It was a sharp-nosed,

EARLY MAMMALS

Ichthyornis

long-tailed, ratlike little beast with skin that was covered with hair instead of scales. Its whole body was not as long as one of the dinosaur's teeth, and the big reptile probably did not even notice it. But in a few million years, this insignificant little animal's descendants would be the new owners of the earth; and the dinosaurs and most of the other reptiles would be gone forever! For the little beast was a mammal—an ancestor of the great family of mammals that fills the world today. That family includes dogs, cats, horses, cows, camels, elephants, bears, dolphins, and *us*—human beings.

Tyrannosaurus Rex

How was it possible for these little furry beasts to take over the world from the dinosaurs? How was it possible for them to change into so many different things? The answer to that lies in the word *evolution*— the name we have given to the force of nature that causes living things to change slowly, over many millions of years, until they are completely different from their ancestors.

When an animal is changed by evolution, it is often made better able to survive than its ancestors were. Such was the case with mammals. The ancestors of the mammals were one group of *reptiles,* and the mammals were an improvement over them.

Reptiles have certain problems. For one thing, they are cold-blooded. This means their bodies get just as hot or as cold as the air around them. If a reptile is in a hot, sunny place, such as a desert, its body soaks up the heat. The reptile could get so hot that its blood would literally boil. The reptile must get rid of some of the heat by moving into shade or into water and staying there until it cools off. And if the air becomes cold, as often happens at night, the reptile's body cools off until the reptile becomes stiff and slow-moving. Then it must warm up by lying in sunshine until it can move easily again. Reptiles often have to spend a lot of time either cooling off or warming up!

Mammals don't have this problem. Their furry, warm-blooded bodies are able to adjust to heat or cold automatically. If a mammal gets too hot, it pants or sweats, bringing water out of its body. When the water evaporates, it carries heat with it and the mammal is cooled. In cold surroundings, on the other hand, a mammal's fur helps it keep warm by trapping air next to the skin. A mammal can also warm up by shivering or by moving rapidly. Because a mammal's body can adjust this way, its body temperature always stays about the same.

So, thanks to evolution a mammal doesn't have to lie still and wait to cool off or warm up as a reptile does. And this is a big improvement. A mammal can keep right on hunting for food, digging a shelter, or doing whatever it wants, while its body takes care of heat and cold automatically.

Another difference between mammals and reptiles is the way they're born and the way they get food as babies. Most reptile mothers lay eggs and then just wander away, leaving the eggs to hatch out by themselves. The eggs are usually unprotected. They can be eaten by animals, stepped on and crushed, covered up by sandstorms. If the eggs do hatch, the reptile babies must start right out hunting for food for themselves. They're on their own.

But again, the way mammals are born is an improvement. Mammal babies don't come out of eggs; they grow inside their mothers' bodies, safe and protected until they are born. Then, unlike reptile babies that have to start hunting food, mammal babies are fed by their mothers. The food of all baby mammals is milk that is made inside the mother's body and comes out of openings called *mammae.* It is from that word that the name *mammal* comes.

Of course, none of these differences came

Present-day Lizard

about quickly. The reptiles that were the mammals' ancestors changed a little at a time, over millions of years. First, their teeth and their digestive systems changed, so that they were able to chew their food better and get more energy from it. This helped them become warm-blooded. Their scales slowly changed to hairs, for that's what a hair is—a scale that has been changed by evolution. Sweat glands formed in their skins. Later, in some of the females, sweat glands evolved into milk glands— mammae. Most of these evolving creatures continued to lay eggs. But in time some stopped laying eggs. They gave birth to live young.

Those first "true" mammals—furry and warm-blooded and giving birth to live babies that they fed with milk—probably appeared in the world between 150 million and 100 million years ago. And this was right at the time when the great dinosaurs ruled the earth. So for millions of years mammals shared the swamps and forests with the dinosaurs. Those first kinds of mammals were tiny, ratlike beasts only a few inches long. They ate insects and probably fruit, seeds, buds, worms, and the flesh of dead animals they found. They probably weren't as smart or as quick moving as most of the mammals of today, but they were smarter and quicker than most reptiles, and well able to hold their own in a world that reptiles ruled.

Millions of years rolled by, and the Age of Reptiles came to an end. For reasons we don't know, the dinosaurs and other big reptiles died out. Now, the world became a good place for the little furry beasts. And evolution continued its work, changing them into many different forms. The Age of Mammals had begun.

The Age of Mammals has been going on for about 70 million years. Many different kinds of furry beasts have come and gone during all those years. You will read about some of those strange, ancient mammals in this book. We know a lot about these beasts, from their fossil skeletons and their similarities to modern mammals. But there are still many things we don't know for sure. The stories about the animals in this book are based on the beliefs of many scientists as to how the animals may have lived, but it's important to remember that many details of those beliefs are based on little more than guesswork. For many of those ancient mammals, such as the huge "thunder beast," the "shovel-tusked" elephant, and the puzzling Arsinoitherium, were not really quite like any animals living now. If it weren't for their fossil bones, preserved for millions of years, we might never have known that such creatures ever lived.

Oxyeana

Eohippus — THE DAWN HORSE

IT WAS DAWN over the North America of 55 million years ago. At the eastern horizon, the red morning sun was creeping into the sky, driving out night's blackness and covering up the stars. As the ruddy light moved across them, the green, swampy forests and rolling uplands waked into life. Bird voices screeched, twittered, and quacked. Insects, warmed into activity after the night's coolness, filled the air with chirps, creaks, and buzzes. The creatures of the night retreated into their dens and holes, and the creatures of day set out upon the important business of finding food.

In a broad glade in a great forest, a herd of animals had begun their morning feeding. They were dainty creatures, no bigger than house cats, with slender legs and little feet with spreading toes. There were four toes on their front feet, and three on the back ones, and on each toe was a tiny hoof. The animals' tails were longish and stout, and their backs were high and curved, like the backs of rabbits. Their heads were rather deerlike. They certainly didn't look much like horses. But that's what they were —the first true horses, ancestors of the horses of today. Their official name is *Hyracotherium,* but many people prefer to call them by the name *Eohippus,* which means "dawn horse."

Modern horses are grazers, grass eaters. But there wasn't much grass in the world of 55 million years ago, and even if there had been, little Eohippus couldn't have eaten it, for its teeth weren't strong enough to chew such tough vegetation. These first little horses were browsers that lived in forests and fed on soft, juicy leaves, tender buds, and pulpy fruits.

Hours passed and the sun slowly rose higher. The little horses had nearly finished their feeding. Shortly, they would troop to the nearest pool for a long, satisfying drink. Then they would seek places in the deep shade of the woods, where they would lie hidden until the forest became filled with late afternoon shadows. The horses would come forth to browse again for a while in the hours before sundown.

Suddenly, from out of the forest that surrounded the glade, a pair of monsters emerged. They strode on two powerful legs that ended in sharp-taloned three-toed feet with heel-like back appendages. Red eyes gleamed, and wickedly curved beaks jutted out of their big, feathered heads. They were giant birds, taller than a tall man, and they

Diatryma

EOHIPPUS

Eohippus   Orohippus   Mesohippus   Merychippus   Present-day Horse

were flesh-eating killers.

At the first glimpse of these two enemies, the horses exploded into flight, rushing in terror for the far end of the glade. They moved swiftly—but the giant birds could move swiftly, too. Their wings were useless for flying, but their legs were made for running. Feet drumming on the ground, they sped after the horses, their bodies bent far forward and their small wings spread out for balance. A sharp beak stabbed out savagely, closing around a little horse's back. The bird that had made a successful catch stopped and began to eat. The other bird pursued the horses on into the forest. . . .

Eohippus and the giant bird, which is called *Diatryma,* were both natives of the western part of North America, about where the states of Wyoming and New Mexico are today. But Eohippus wasn't strictly an American animal; fossil skeletons of these little creatures have been found in Europe, too.

But although we know very little about Eohippus's ancestor, we know a great deal about its descendants. The history of the horse family is probably the best known of all animal histories and is one of the best proofs of evolution, the process that causes animals to change their shapes and ways of life over many millions of years.

About 10 million years or so after the time of Eohippus came a horse that has been named *Orohippus.* It was a little larger than the cat-sized Eohippus, its head was more horselike in appearance, and its teeth were different. But it still had toes on its feet, as Eohippus did. When Orohippus first appeared on the scene, it lived in swampy forests, but near the end of its time on earth it moved out onto the grassy plains that were gradually taking over large parts of the world. It probably was beginning to eat grass instead of leaves.

Ten million more years passed, and the land changed. Most of the swampy forests had dried up and vanished completely, and enormous grass-filled plains now covered much of North America. A descendant of Eohippus called *Mesohippus* lived at this time. It was about the size of a police dog and looked much more like a horse than either of its ancestors, Eohippus or Orohippus, had. All of its feet had three toes with hoofs on them, but the middle toes and hoofs were much larger than the others. Mesohippus was becoming a one-toed animal like the modern horse. And, like the modern horse, it was strictly a grass eater.

Another 10 million or so years later— about 25 million years from our time— came *Merychippus,* which was about the size of a calf. Merychippus still had three toes on each foot, but two of the toes had become small, while on each foot the middle toe and its hoof had grown longer and much larger. The result was that Merychippus walked on only one toe on each foot, just as modern horses do, for its other side toes didn't even touch the ground. Merychippus probably looked so much like a modern horse that had you seen it galloping across an ancient prairie you might have said, "Look at the little pony!"

With the passage of many millions of

Evolution of Forefoot

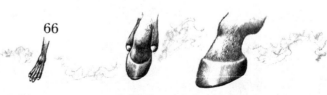

Eohippus   Merychippus   Present-day Horse

years more, horses grew slowly larger while their useless "leftover" toes continued to become smaller. Finally, about a million years ago, the kind of horse we now have appeared in the world.

All this took place in North America. The little European Eohippus had a number of descendants, too, but for some reason they all died off. By about 30 million years ago there were no horses of any kind in Europe.

Thirty million years ago, North America was an island continent, entirely surrounded by water, as Australia is now. But off and on during the millions of years between that time and this one, earthquakes and volcanoes caused "land bridges" to push up out of the ocean. These bridges connected the western part of North America to Asia, and the southern part of North America to South America. Horses migrated over the bridges west into Asia and Europe and south into Central and South America. (A lot of other kinds of animals used the bridges, too). So horses reappeared in Europe and began to do very well there. They also seemed to be doing very well in South America.

Then about 25 thousand years ago, something mysterious happened in North and South America. All the horses in those countries—and a number of other kinds of animals, as well—became extinct. Why this happened is a puzzle that scientists have not been able to figure out. But at any rate, there were no horses left anywhere in the western hemisphere. About 500 years ago Spanish explorers brought horses with them from Europe, and so horses were reintroduced into the western world.

Since the time of little Eohippus, 55 million years ago, there have been herds of wild horses by the millions, often on several different continents at the same time. Today, the zebras of Africa, small herds of wild asses, and a very small group of Asiatic horses (called Pryzewalski's Horse) are the only wild descendants left of the little dawn horse. There are probably just a few hundred thousand of these wild members of the horse family, altogether. Although there are many other horses in the world, they are all tame creatures that have become the servants of an animal that wasn't even around in Eohippus's day—the animal called man.

Brontotherium — THE THUNDER BEAST

THOUSANDS OF YEARS ago, when bands of Indians hunted among the hills and prairies of what is now South Dakota and Nebraska, they sometimes came across huge bones lying in gullies and ravines. The bones were not those of any animal the Indians had ever seen; they were far too big and thick to belong to even so large a beast as a bison. Usually, the bones were found only after there had been a heavy downpour of rain, so the Indians felt that rainstorms were somehow responsible for the bones being there.

A legend grew that the bones belonged to huge animals that lived in the sky. The Indians believed that the animals leaped down to earth during rainstorms, and that thunder was the sound of their big hoofs thudding into the ground when they landed. The Indians called these legendary beasts "thunder horses."

The bones were really fossil bones, of course—bones of real animals that had lived many millions of years ago. Heavy rains sometimes washed the bones out of their resting places in the sides of ravines, which was why they were usually found only after severe storms. But the Indians had no way of knowing about such things

as fossils. When the great fossil hunter Professor Othniel Marsh discovered many of these bones nearly a century ago, he remembered the old Indian legend of the thunder horses, and he named the prehistoric animal *Brontotherium,* which means "thunder beast."

The thunder beast was a massive, hulking animal. A tall man's head would not have reached to its shoulders. It was a good 8 feet high and nearly 15 feet long. It had thick, heavy legs and broad, spread-out feet to support the weight of a big, bulky body that weighed more than that of most elephants. Its rhinoceroslike head was rather small for such a massive body.

On its nose, the thunder beast had a thick, blunt horn, shaped like the letter Y. It used that horn in many ways. It undoubtedly fought other brontotheres to prove its superiority. It probably fought to defend its territory. And it may have used its heavy horn to protect its youngsters from the prowling, wolflike flesh eaters that were around in those days. To use its horn, the big beast must have lowered its head, nose to the ground, so that the horn jutted straight out. Then, with big feet drumming on the ground and

Poëbrotherium

big body moving with surprising speed, it charged. The flesh eater that couldn't scramble out of the way in time was lifted up on the horn, and tossed high into the air with enough force to smash its bones when it hit the ground. Male brontotheres probably also used their horns to fight each other at times, too. Their horns were bigger than those of the females.

Today, the land through which the thunder beast once roamed has become wheat-filled farmland, pasture, and eroded ridges of clay and sandstone. But when the brontotheres were alive, they ambled about on moist, grassy plains dotted with water holes and dense clumps of trees and bushes. Surrounding the plains were mountain ridges, among which the cones of volcanoes often pointed upward at the sky.

Above one of the volcanoes that overlooked such a plain, on a day more than 40 million years ago, there hung a great, umbrella-shaped cloud of black, almost solid-looking smoke. From time to time the volcano rumbled ominously. The animals that made their home on the plain were restless, as if they sensed that the rumbles were a warning of danger. that might leap out upon them at any moment. A large herd of three-toed horses the size of police dogs browsed upon the plain, as did a herd of sheep-sized, humpless camels. Doglike and catlike flesh eaters prowled in the tall grass or lay in ambush among the thickets.

In one of the many water holes, a group of brontotheres were soaking themselves, enjoying the coolness of the water on their tough, thick hides. A few of the big animals were nosing about in the bushes at the edge of the hole, seeking soft, juicy leaves of the kind that were their main food.

Suddenly, there was a sound—a muffled roar that slowly grew louder, like the noise of a swiftly approaching subway train. The ground beneath the brontotheres' feet began to quiver and shake. Then there was an ear-splitting explosion from the volcano. The entire plain shuddered violently, throwing even the big brontotheres to their knees. Red flames shot up from the volcano's cone, and the black cloud of smoke began to spread out over the plain, blotting out the sun, turning the sky as dark as a moonless night.

A shower of hot, wet ashes and chunks of steaming rock began to pour down upon the plain, hurled out of the volcano by the explosion. A sharp stench of burning sulfur filled the air. Confused and excited by the noise and the bits of rock pelting them, the brontotheres charged out of the water and milled about, bellowing.

With a titanic blast, the volcano blew itself into fragments. Out of the crater that was left poured a great, glowing, fiery flood that rushed down toward the plain—*liquid rock* from the earth's interior, rock so hot that it boiled and flowed like thick syrup! The plain that had been veiled in blackness moments before now became lit with a hellish orange glare.

At the sight of the river of fire rolling toward them, the animals of the plain bolted in terror. Plant eaters and flesh eaters ran side by side, their enmity forgotten in the face of the thing they all feared most of all. The brontotheres, too, were overcome with terror and joined the other creatures in flight. Big feet thudding, they galloped wildly in search of safety. . . .

The time during which the brontotheres lived was one of volcanic activity. That doesn't mean that volcanoes erupted every year, or even every 10 or 20 years. But we do know that there were volcanic eruptions where brontotheres lived, and the big beasts must have sometimes been terrorized by them.

Brontotheres, often known as titanotheres, meaning "giant beasts," descended from a little animal about the size of a small dog. Descendants of that small creature got bigger and bigger.

Brontotheres were the biggest members of the family, but they were also the last, because all the brontotheres living in North America and Asia died out about 35 million years ago. That was the end of the *Titanotherium* family. You could hardly call them "successful" animals, because they were around for only about 20 million years. That may seem like a long time, but

it isn't really. Many mammal families, such as horses, camels, and elephants, have been going strong for more than 50 million years. And turtles, horseshoe crabs, and many other kinds of creatures have been around for *hundreds* of millions of years.

It's hard to say why the thunder beasts became extinct. Some scientists think they may have been slow witted. But other even more slow-witted animals than they have survived. The last of the thunder beasts lived at a time when the climate was becoming drier, and grass was spreading through the world, crowding out the soft, leafy plants that needed lots of moisture, and that were the brontotheres' food. Perhaps the big beasts just couldn't adapt quickly enough to this change.

There is no animal quite like the thunder beast or any of the other titanotheres anywhere today. They were distantly related to horses, rhinoceroses, and tapirs, but were nevertheless a completely different kind of animal. And when they became extinct, their kind of animal was gone from the world forever.

Rhinoceros

Tapir

Comparative Size of Brontotherium and Present-day Animals

Smilodon — THE SABER-TOOTHED CAT

A MILLION years ago, the western part of the United States was as filled with animals as a game preserve in Africa is today. Herds of horses, humpless camels, and big elephants with curved tusks roamed the yellow-green plains, where they were hunted by big cats and packs of pony-sized wolves. Great, shaggy ground sloths lumbered among the thickets, and giant beavers the size of small bears skillfully built dams in streams and rivers. Huge vultures perched in the trees, scanning the countryside with sharp, red eyes. They were waiting for some animal to kill another and eat its fill, after which they would move in on the dead carcass and pick its bones clean.

A number of these animals were moving about near a small water hole early one afternoon. Camels, elephants, and sloths were all minding their own business and intent only on filling their stomachs with the grass, leaves, or other plants that were their food. Unknown to them, another animal was also present, and it, too, was intent on filling its stomach. A big, catlike creature was lying hidden in the tall grass at the edge of the water hole, motionless except for a nervous twitching of its tail. The cat was much like a tiger in shape, but was more heavily built, and the gently waving tail was shorter and stubbier than that of a tiger.

There was another difference, too. When a tiger's mouth is closed, its teeth can't be seen. This big cat's mouth was closed, but two of its teeth were distinctly visible. Curving down out of the cat's upper lip, on each side of its mouth, were 6-inch-long, wickedly sharp fangs. They were slightly flattened and curved, and resembled nothing so much as the old-fashioned kind of sword called a saber. Running down the length of the backs of those fangs were tiny serrations like the teeth on a saw.

Eyes fixed unwaveringly on the water hole, the saber-toothed cat waited patiently. The ambush was perfect. The cat was completely hidden and the wind was blowing toward it from the water hole, so that no scent could be detected by any animal passing in front of the hiding place.

But the cat was detected—from above. A shadow flickered over the saber-tooth's body as a big vulture wheeled overhead. The bird sailed to the branch of a nearby tree, closed its wings, and perched with long, scrawny neck thrust forward. From the air the vulture had seen the big cat lying in

SMILODON

Mastodon

Giant Vulture

72

ambush. The vulture had learned early that it had only to stay near such flesh eaters and it, too, would eventually have food —the remains of the flesh eater's kill. So with a patience that matched that of the saber-tooth, the vulture waited.

A group of camels came down to the water hole to drink. When the cat saw them, its tail moved a little faster, but it made no attempt to attack. It could run fast only for a short distance, and by the time it launched itself into a charge, the fleet-footed camels would be galloping to safety. The saber-tooth wanted slower prey, which it could leap on and dispatch quickly. It continued to wait.

Time passed. Then, a measured tread shook the ground. Some big, heavy—and slow—creatures were approaching the water hole.

They were mastodons, a small herd of great, gray animals with enormous curved tusks. And one of them was a calf.

The adult mastodons waded into the water, dunking their trunks and sucking water into them, then coiling their trunks up to squirt water into their open mouths. But the calf wasn't yet interested in quenching its thirst. It strayed a little distance from the others, trunk questing here and there in the tall grass. Perhaps it smelled something, or perhaps it had seen something that made it curious. The little mastodon took a step, then another. Each step brought it closer to the motionless, hidden cat.

Abruptly, as if losing interest, the calf turned to rejoin the herd. As it did so, the saber-tooth rose smoothly to its feet and took two bounds that brought it smashing down onto the calf's back. The cat's mouth opened—not the way a modern lion or tiger's mouth opens, but in a tremendous gape, with the lower jaw dropping straight down and back, nearly flat against the throat. Like a striking snake, the cat's head stabbed down, burying the long, saberlike teeth in the young mastodon's neck. With a single squeal of shock, the calf crumpled onto its side in the grass.

From the water hole there was a trumpeted scream of fury. Several of the mastodons had witnessed the attack on the calf, and they came charging out of the water, trunks curled back over their heads, eyes blazing. The cat whirled and streaked for safety, zigzagging through the grass with the great beasts thudding in pursuit. They chased it for several hundred yards, then one slowed to a stop and turned back, and the others followed.

The calf lay unmoving, blood welling up from the horrible wounds in its neck and staining the grass crimson. Slowly, the herd gathered around the slain youngster. Several of the mastodons eased their trunks under its body as if trying to lift it back onto its feet and coax it to return to life.

Staying under cover, the saber-tooth slunk back to within 50 or 60 yards of the mastodons and lay down in the grass, watching them. For several hours, the mastodons stayed near the dead calf, rocking their big bodies from side to side, uttering rumbles and squeals. Finally, with the afternoon sun low and red in the sky, they turned and trailed away as if admitting at last that the calf was truly dead and there was nothing they could do.

The saber-tooth watched them carefully, but they paid it no further attention. When they were well in the distance, the cat rose to its feet and paced to the body. It began feeding. From the tree, the vulture, which had been joined by others, watched.

When the cat had filled itself to satisfaction, it padded to the water hole and drank noisily, taking in big gulps of water with a ribbonlike tongue. Then, turning away, it prowled off in search of a place to sleep. It would sleep for many hours and awaken hungry to hunt again for another meal. Such was the way of its life.

As the saber-tooth moved away from its kill, the vultures rose from the trees with a great clamor and rustle and swept toward the carcass. Now it was their turn to eat.

The saber-toothed cat has been named *Smilodon,* which means "knife tooth." It lived from about 1 million years ago until about 20 thousand years ago.

Was it much like a modern lion or tiger? It was about the same size, but it was a heavier and probably slower animal. Because of the size of its brain, some scientists think it was not as intelligent as a modern lion, tiger, or even a house cat. Others think it probably was.

Did it have a mane? Was it striped like a tiger, or spotted like a leopard? There's no way to tell, for sure. And was it really the terrible killer that its saberlike teeth seem to indicate? Many scientists think so, but some aren't so sure. They think it may have lived mainly on the bodies of dead animals that it happened to find, just as vultures do.

Whatever its way of life, Smilodon and other saber-toothed cats like it were widespread throughout the world. But by about 20 thousand years ago, they had all become extinct. There are no saber-toothed cats anywhere in the world today.

Present-day Sloth

Megatherium — THE GIANT SLOTH

IN THE FORESTS of South America there lives a little animal called a sloth. Its body is covered with shaggy fur, and its ears and tail are so tiny they can't even be seen. On all four of its feet are long, curling claws, like hooks, that fit neatly around tree branches. The sloth spends nearly its whole life upside down, hanging by its claws from branches, moving along each branch with incredible slowness as it feeds on leaves and buds. From its blunt nose to the invisible tail, the sloth is only about 2 feet long.

About 30 thousand years ago there was another kind of sloth living in South America and the southernmost part of North America. A relative of the little tree sloth, it lived on the ground instead of up in trees. And it wasn't just 2 feet long; it was as big as an elephant! Because of its size, this sloth of long ago has been named *Megatherium,* meaning "giant beast."

Unlike the nearly tailless little tree sloth, Megatherium had a long, enormously thick tail that tapered to a blunt point. But in most other ways the giant sloth was quite a bit like its tiny, modern relative. It, too, had long, curling claws on its feet. But because of those claws it couldn't put its feet down flat when it walked; it lumbered along on

the knuckles of its front feet and the sides of its back ones. This probably caused it to shuffle clumsily.

Like its relative, Megatherium was also covered with shaggy fur. But beneath the fur, imbedded in its skin, were many knobby "pebbles" of bone. This was a kind of armor that somewhat protected the giant sloth from flesh eaters. For in spite of its size, the young megathere was probably preyed upon by the savage saber-toothed cats that prowled in parts of the world at that time. The sloth was not completely helpless against these marauders, however, for while it used its claws mainly for digging and for pulling tree branches to its mouth, they were also vicious weapons. A single swing of one of those big, clawed paws smashing against an enemy's body would have crunched bones and left terrible, bloody wounds.

Much of what we know about giant ground sloths was learned from fossil bones of the big animals. Bones of *Paramylodon* (another genus of large ground sloth) and of many other mammals and birds have been taken out of the famous La Brea tar pits in Los Angeles, California. And similar tar pits in Peru preserve many kinds of fos-

76

sils, including Megatherium itself. Tar pits, formed where oil oozes out of the ground, were a death trap for thousands of creatures.

We can easily imagine a mylodont or a megathere becoming a victim of the tar pits. On a morning 30 thousand years ago, the sun rose redly over a countryside of broad, grassy plains dotted with clumps of trees and bushes. It glinted on the dew-covered, golden-brown fur of the enormous, shaggy beast that lay sleeping, curled into a great ball in the middle of a grove of trees.

A fly, roused to activity by the morning warmth, came to rest on the ground sloth's nose. After a moment, the big animal's nostrils twitched and its eyes blinked open. The fly darted away.

The sloth's mouth gaped open in a huge yawn. Then it snorted, and lurching to its feet, ambled off, nose close to the ground in search of an interesting smell that had suddenly caught its attention. It paused where the smell was strongest and began to dig with its claws. Shortly, it uncovered the tasty roots of a clump of wild onions and began to munch on them with immense satisfaction.

After it finished, and when no more interesting smells could be detected, the giant sloth turned back toward the grove. Making its slow way to the nearest tree, it suddenly reared up, supporting its weight on its back legs and thick, muscular tail. In this position, its head was among the lower branches of the tree, a good 15 feet off the ground. Reaching up, it hooked its claws around a branch and began to feed. Its long, tubular tongue stretched forth and,

almost like a tentacle, wrapped itself around clusters of leaves, stripping them from the branch and carrying them into the sloth's mouth.

The sloth fed for nearly an hour, moving from one tree to another. At last it was satisfied and dropped its front legs back onto the ground with a thump. Then, with its peculiar waddling walk, it shuffled off across the grassy landscape.

The plain abounded with many kinds of animals, but the hulking sloth ignored them, as they did it. It passed a large herd of zebralike animals grazing placidly, and a little later encountered a small group of mammoths. Once, it passed within a few yards of a saber-toothed cat that had recently fed and lay resting, but alert, hidden by the tall grass. Had the cat been hungry, the sloth might have been in for trouble.

The sun was high in the sky now, flooding the plain with heat, and the sloth began to feel thirsty. It quickened its pace, turning its big head from side to side, searching for the telltale gleam of water. After a time, as it crossed a slight rise in the ground, it caught sight of a large sheet of silver, sparkling enticingly in the sunlight.

Near the water there was a peculiar tang in the air, a sharp, unfamiliar, oily smell. It was not the smell of an animal, so it meant nothing to the sloth. The big beast merely snorted, to clear the acrid odor from its nostrils, and plodded to the edge of the water, its feet sinking squishily into the ground.

The water at the edge of the pool was

78

just a thin film, so the sloth moved farther out. With each step its feet sank deeper, and it was harder to pull them loose. Suddenly, the sloth couldn't move at all! The pool of water was really a deep pool of black, sticky tar, covered with only a thin coat of oily water.

Not understanding what was happening to it, the giant sloth tried to pull first one foot loose, then another. Its movements only made it sink deeper, until its legs and belly were completely immersed in the treacherous tar. Completely helpless, the big beast suddenly sensed its terrible predicament and began to wallow in panic, straining its body and making terrified noises.

Soon, only the sloth's head was above the tar. Its eyes rolled wildly, and it stretched its neck, desperately trying to snatch a few more seconds of life. But the very weight of its own big body continued to pull it down. Slowly, its head went under. Tar filled its nose and mouth and death came quickly.

The sloth's body continued to sink into the sticky blackness, and after a time its skin and flesh rotted away. Thirty thousand or more years after its death, its bones, and those of many other animals, were discovered by workmen as they were removing tar from the pit to use for paving roads.

Our knowledge of giant sloths doesn't all come from just their bones, however. In a cave in South America and in caves in North America's Southwest, fragments of the skin and hair of giant sloths have been found, marvelously preserved by the dry air. From these fragments, scientists learned about the color and texture of Megatherium's fur, and about the pebbly, bone armor that was imbedded in its skin.

Those fragments of skin and hair also told us something else—that giant sloths have not been extinct for very long. Scientists feel sure that these huge, shaggy, elephant-sized animals of the prehistoric world were still lumbering about in South America no more than a few hundred years ago!

But today, the only sloths in South America are the little 2-foot-long tree sloths, hanging upside down among the leafy branches.

Glyptodon—A MAMMAL WITH A SHELL

ONE MILLION years ago, a great grassy plain covered much of the southern part of South America. It was almost as flat and even as a tabletop, stretching away on all sides under a wide open sky. Giant thistles grew thickly among the pampas grass, and their pale, purple flowers, nodding above the grass tops, made the plain look as if it were coated with a lavender haze. When the wind blew, the tall tassels of grass and the spiky heads of the thistles swirled and swayed, so that whole sections of the land seemed to be running away in front of the breeze.

The late afternoon sun hung low in the sky over the great plain, tinting it orange and casting patches of purple shadow. The vast carpet of grass appeared to be empty of life. But abruptly, there was movement. Something rose up out of the grass and began to follow a slow zigzag course with many pauses. From a distance it looked like nothing so much as a big, dome-shaped boulder lurching through the grass all by itself!

It was an animal whose body was covered with a great, humped, turtlelike shell. It was not a turtle, however, for its small, roundish head and the portions of its feet

that peeped out from under the shell were furry—a sure sign that the beast was a mammal. It was about 9 feet long from nose to tail, and its shell was nearly 4 feet high. Its legs were stout, with short, stubby toes and thick, blunt claws. It was an animal that has been named *Glyptodon*.

An enormous number of animals swarmed through the vast sea of grass where Glyptodon lived. For most of them, life was simply a matter of keeping one leap ahead of some other animal's hungry mouth, for they were all part of the great food chain of the grassland. By the millions, tiny, many-legged creatures—the insects that crawled and hunted and fed and laid their eggs among the stalks of grass—became food for other insects, for birds, and for little mouselike mammals. And those animals, in their turn, were preyed on by snakes, larger birds, and larger mammals. Not even the biggest animals could escape from the food chain. The huge, shaggy, elephant-sized sloths that shuffled ponderously about on the plain were often pulled down by the tigerlike saber-toothed cats that prowled through the grass. The toxodonts—short-legged, big-headed animals that looked somewhat like 9-foot-long

Toxodon

Ankylosaurus

guinea pigs with tusks—were prized food for many hungry flesh eaters.

But chances are that Glyptodon did not have much to fear from other creatures. It was not a fierce animal that could defend itself with sharp teeth and claws, and it certainly wasn't a swift runner, able to outdistance the flesh eaters, but it was well protected by its bony shell. Also, it had a "secret weapon."

Glyptodon was a relative of the animals called armadillos that live today in South and Central America and in the southern part of North America. There are several kinds of armadillos, but they all have bony shells covering their bodies. These shells aren't stiff, like turtle shells; they're movable. One kind of armadillo can curl itself up when it is in danger, tucking its tail, paws, and nose into its shell. This turns it into a hard, bony ball that most animals cannot bite. Another kind of armadillo can quickly dig itself into the ground and wedge itself in so that nothing is exposed but its hard, bone-covered back.

But Glyptodon did not use either of these two methods of defense. It had what may have been a better way of defending itself. Its shell was thick and stiff and rock-hard; it had a kind of "helmet" of thick bone on the top of its head; and its thick, heavy tail was covered with knobby bumps of bone. So when Glyptodon was in danger it simply crouched down and lowered its head. Its feet were then covered completely by the shell, and the only part of its head that showed was the part covered by the bony cap. In this position, Glyptodon was noth-

ing but a big, round dome of rock-hard bone—not at all the sort of thing that a saber-toothed cat or a wolf would want to sink its fangs into.

Of course, Glyptodon's bone-covered tail was not covered by the shell. And that hard tail was Glyptodon's secret weapon—a war club. Glyptodon could swing it, suddenly and savagely, to smash it into the body of a wolf or cat that was snuffling about too closely. One kind of Glyptodon even had a big cluster of sharp, bony spikes on the tip of its tail, like the war club called a mace that knights of long ago used in their battles.

With its bony armor shell, Glyptodon was, of course, very much like a turtle. It was also a lot like another kind of animal that had lived many millions of years earlier, a dinosaur called *Ankylosaurus*. Ankylosaurus, too, was covered with bony armor and had a knobby, spiky tail that it could use as a war club. Yet Glyptodon was not at all closely related to either of these two creatures. Turtles are reptiles. Ankylosaurus was also. Glyptodon was, of course, a mammal. But they are all so much alike that it's easy to see how Nature often repeats ways of helping living things take care of themselves.

What did Glyptodon eat, and what sort of life did it live? It belonged to the group of animals called "edentates," a group that includes armadillos, sloths, and anteaters. *Edentata* means "without teeth," but actually, most of these animals do have teeth, although their teeth are often nothing more than rather weak pegs. Glyptodon's teeth

82

Doedicurus

show that it couldn't have been a flesh eater but perhaps it wasn't just a plant eater, either. Its relatives, the armadillos, eat lots of insects, grubs, and worms, and a few kinds of berries, so perhaps Glyptodon's diet was somewhat like theirs.

Glyptodon probably didn't live the same sort of life that its armadillo cousins do, though. Most armadillos are great diggers and make burrows for themselves in which they hide and sleep. But Glyptodon's blunt claws must not have been much good for digging, and with its stiff, turtlelike shell it wouldn't have been able to move around in a burrow very easily. Glyptodon may have just wandered about on the grasslands and the edges of deserts, looking for the things it ate and squatting down inside its armored shell whenever it encountered a flesh-eating animal that began to show too much hungry interest in it.

Glyptodon seems to have started out in South America about 50 million years ago.

At first it was a little creature, much like an armadillo, but as millions of years passed, it got bigger and bigger and its movable, armadillolike shell changed into a stiff, bony dome. By about 1 million years ago, this large, bony-armored animal was living in the grasslands and prairies throughout South and Central America and the southern parts of North America.

Despite its long history and apparently successful way of defending itself, Glyptodon became extinct by about 25 thousand years ago. It left no descendants or relatives of any kind. Fortunately there are still armadillos in the world to help us understand what kind of an animal Glyptodon was, for otherwise this unusual beast would have posed a real problem for scientists. Except for the armadillos, no mammal living today has bony armor on its body. So who could have imagined a creature such as Glyptodon—a furry mammal in a turtle shell!

Present-day Armadillo

Mammoth—THE FURRY ELEPHANT

THE LAND was flat and gray-green beneath a sullen gray sky. A biting wind rushed over the ground, rattling the few stunted bushes that huddled here and there on the landscape. It was autumn on the tundra, the great barren plain that lies between the ever-frozen north polar lands and the huge evergreen forest that stretches across the northern part of the world. Soon, the ground that had thawed to a depth of a few inches during the brief spring and summer would be frozen ironhard again and covered with a heavy, white blanket of snow.

Out of the northern horizon came a cluster of dark, shaggy shapes. They moved with ponderous majesty, heads nodding, trunks curling and uncurling. They were very much like modern elephants, but their backs and heads were higher and rounder, and their ears much smaller than those of an elephant. And they were completely covered with thick, reddish-brown hair. They were mammoths.

It was a small herd of only seven adults and two young calves. The calves looked like fat, fuzzy balls, and their tusks were still short and only slightly curved. The tusks of the older beasts formed great

C-shaped curves. In winter, those thick, curved tusks helped the mammoths get their food. When the animals lowered their heads and rolled them from side to side, their curved tusks scooped away the snow, enabling them to reach the grass and moss beneath.

But food was no problem, yet. As the mammoths plodded along in their slow, stately fashion, their hairy trunks coiled down to pluck up herbs, flowers, clumps of moss, and tufts of grass. The tips of their trunks, which of course were their noses, were much like modern elephants' trunks. There was a kind of muscular "finger" above the nostrils and a thick flap below that could be used almost like a hand.

The leader of the herd, a 10-foot-tall male, came to the steep bank of a stream. He turned aside, following the course of the stream toward the great fir forest that loomed like a dim green cloud far in the distance on the southern horizon. Silently, the others swung into line behind him, the two calves close to their mothers.

For many years, the river bank at this point had been crumbling away as the melting snow each spring had swollen the stream, turning it for a time into a swift-

moving flood. Now, a large section of the bank was ready to collapse entirely. And it was on this section that the last mammoth in the line, a young male, chanced to put his full weight.

Suddenly, the bank gave way beneath him. He dropped like a stone, 20 feet into the shallow water and mud of the stream, landing in a sitting position with a smashing shock that broke his hip and right foreleg. A torrent of mud and icy earth poured down around him as a great section of the bank collapsed completely. The mammoth had time for only a quick squeal of pain and terror before he was completely buried under several tons of muck.

He struggled in panic, but the soft mud held him, and his broken bones would not permit him to move. Unable to fight his way free, he was dead of suffocation in minutes.

The young mammoth's squeal had startled the rest of the herd. They stopped short at the sound, then quickly bunched together, peering about for signs of danger and emitting rumbles and squeals of worry. Their eyesight was not very keen, but their sense of smell was excellent, and it told them no other animals were nearby. But they sensed that something had happened and were puzzled and disturbed by the disappearance of one of their companions. The old leader pointed his trunk into the air and screamed out a call. Then, dropping his trunk, he stood shifting his big body from side to side as if anxiously awaiting an answer.

After several minutes he seemed to come to a decision, and turning, plodded once more on his way. The others followed. But from time to time one of them would break stride and swing around to trumpet shrilly, as if seeking sight or sound of the missing young male. Worried and uneasy, the animals moved on toward the distant forest, leaving far behind them the river bank where the young mammoth lay buried.

Days passed. The sky grew ever darker and the wind more piercingly cold. The ground began to freeze. In a few weeks it was frozen stone-cold beneath a cover of white snow. And the mammoth's body, in its tomb of ice and earth, was frozen as hard as the ground.

The mammoth lay on the edge of the flood plain near the riverbed, and the bank of the river sloped up more than 20 feet above it. When spring came, melting snow and falling rain washed more dirt down the bank. Some of this was carried away by the river, but some of it piled up on the mammoth's grave, burying the animal deeper. In the cold earth, its body stayed frozen.

Each year, for centuries, more of the river bank eroded away, slipping down to lie on top of the mammoth's grave. Finally, the bank was gone. And with it out of the way, the wind and water were now free to begin their work of eroding the mammoth's grave, carrying dirt away from it a little at a time. After many thousands of springs, the mammoth's body, which had once been deeply buried, was close to the surface.

In the spring of 1900, torrential rains fell, washing away the thawing soil and uncovering frozen soil that thawed and was washed away in its turn. The mammoth's body was uncovered.

In August of that year, a hunter by the name of Semen Tarabykin, with his dog, was tracking an elk near the Berezovka River, in Siberia. Abruptly, the dog swerved, racing off in excitement after a strange, new scent. The dog led Tarabykin to a huge, shaggy body that looked as if it were just crawling out of the earth.

That was the beginning of one of the greatest episodes in the science of zoology. Slowly, word was carried out of the remote Siberian wilderness that the perfectly preserved body of a creature that had vanished from the earth thousands of years before had been discovered.

In May of 1901, when the news reached the Academy of Sciences in St. Petersburg (now called Leningrad), Russia, an expedition set out at once. After a dreadfully difficult journey, the Russian scientists reached the mammoth's body in September.

The body had begun to decay. Worse still, wolves and bears, attracted by the smell, had gnawed away portions of it. At once the scientists began the task of digging the body out of the frozen ground, skinning it, and examining its parts.

The mammoth was a scientific treasure trove. The men found that beneath its long, shaggy hair, it was covered with soft, yellowish fur, like wool, that had helped keep it warm even in the fiercest cold. In its stomach and between its teeth they found remains of the food it had eaten the very day it died. And they found that meat on its back legs was still fresh, tempting them to cook some of the meat and try it. Imagine eating the kind of meat that cavemen had eaten many thousands of years before! But, fearful, they fed it instead to their dogs who gobbled it up gladly.

By mid-October, the work was finished and the expedition returned to St. Petersburg. In the Museum of the Academy of Sciences, the body of the mammoth was stuffed and mounted in exactly the same position it was in when found.

Skeletons of other mammoths, and even portions of mammoths' bodies with skin and fur still on them, have been found in other places since then, for mammoths once lived all over Europe and North America. But it was the Berezovka mammoth that taught us much of what we now know about these ancient members of the elephant family, and that is still regarded as one of the greatest scientific finds of this century.

Ursus Spelaeus—THE GREAT CAVE BEAR

HIGH AMONG the limestone cliffs that overlooked a winding river, a blob of darkness marked the entrance to a cave. Far back within the cave, in a corner where a thin trickle of cold water seeped out of a crack in the limestone, lay a mother cave bear and two cubs.

The mother bear was a big shaggy beast more than 9 feet long and nearly 5 feet high at the shoulders. Her head was massive, and the front part of her body was more powerfully built, and higher, than the back part. When she yawned, she showed the sharp, savage teeth of a meat eater. Yet she ate not only the flesh of animals, but a great many other types of food, as well—berries, nuts, many kinds of leafy plants, insects, seeds. Much of the meat she ate came from the bodies of dead animals she found, which undoubtedly included the giant deer and the woolly rhinoceros. Much food was also provided by many kinds of small creatures such as ground squirrels, frogs, lizards, and fish. But she could also hunt and bring down many larger animals, such as deer and goats.

The mother bear was nervous. For several minutes she had been aware of strange sounds and smells coming from outside the cave. They were unfamiliar sounds and smells, and there was something about them she didn't like. Her lip twitched back in a snarl.

The cave bear didn't know it, but she who had so often been a hunter was now herself being hunted. Her den had been discovered by a party of men searching for food or shelter, and the sounds and smells were coming from them as they made their preparations outside the cave.

These men were short, powerfully built humans with rugged features. In nearly 90 thousands years, when the bones of their kind would first be discovered in a valley in France, they would become known as Neanderthal men. They knew how to make fire and how to make tools and weapons of flaked flint. They probably wore animal-skin garments and spoke a simple language. And they were skillful hunters of the great cave bears.

The bear rose to her feet and paced a few steps forward. A sharp, biting smell was drifting into the cave now. She growled.

Suddenly, a terrific noise broke out outside the cave. The Neanderthal men were shouting at the top of their lungs. Half a dozen flaming branches were hurled into

Giant Deer

88

Woolly Rhinoceros

the cave to lie crackling on the rocky floor, filling the cave with acrid, stinging smoke. The bear snarled. The shouts alarmed and excited her and the flaring torches frightened her. The smoke made her eyes smart and her throat burn. She sensed danger to her cubs from all this sudden noise and activity, and when a she-bear's cubs are threatened, her instincts give her only one course of action. She charges.

With a savage roar, the huge beast rushed out of the cave. Instantly she was pelted with a furious barrage of big, sharp-edged, heavy rocks, hurled down on her by a score of men who had taken positions among the high boulders around the cave's entrance. Ahead of her, a ring of fires blocked her path, and behind them a row of men leaped, howled, and waved burning branches.

Hurt and confused, the bear stopped short, snarling. More rocks rained down on her. One smashed into her head, opening a great cut. Another ripped a deep gash in her back. Thrown torches singed her fur.

Roaring with pain and fury, the bear whirled, trying to get at her attackers, but they were out of reach. A boulder crashed against her snout, blinding her with pain. Whimpering, she dropped into a crouch. One man, more daring than the others, leaped down and drove a spear into her side—a long, straight tree branch that had been sharpened at one end and hardened in fire. With a roar of pain, the bear swung toward him, but he scrambled back up among the boulders.

The bear began to weaken. Bleeding from a score of gashes, bruised and dazed by the rocks that continued to pelt her, and with the spear jutting from her side, her movements grew slower. Grasping their spears firmly, the Neanderthal men began to slip down out of the boulders and close in.

Finally, the great bear lay dead. The Neanderthals clustered about her, gazing at the huge, shaggy form. One man sat gasping on the ground, clutching a gashed arm that had been ripped open by a final swipe of the bear's paw.

One of the men happened to glance toward the cave entrance and gave a grunt, alerting the others. The bear cubs, puzzled and frightened at having been left alone, had worked up their courage to follow their mother and were emerging timidly from the cave. Quickly, several of the hunters moved toward them, and quickly, the cubs joined their mother. The Neanderthals lived in a harsh world where food was often hard to find, and they had little ones of their own to feed. To them, the cubs simply represented more food.

Now the work of skinning and cutting up the great bear began. But first, there was something important the Neanderthals had to do. With their surprisingly sharp stone tools they hacked off the bear's head. Then several of them, one carrying the big head, set out to climb far up to a point near the top of the mountain where there was another cave.

At the cave entrance they lit torches and trooped silently into the gloomy interior. Inside there were several caves connected by narrow passageways. In the passageway between the second and third caves the men halted and piled their torches together on the rocky floor.

The flames flickered redly against a pile of stone slabs that lay at the opening of the third cave. Two of the Neanderthals began to remove slabs from the top of the pile. Shortly, the firelight revealed several gleaming white objects around which the slabs had been placed. These objects were skulls—the skulls of cave bears. Stepping forward, the man who carried the head of the bear that had just been killed placed it among the skulls.

This pile of rocks and cave bear skulls that was made so long ago by Neanderthal hunters was discovered by modern scientists in the cave at the top of Dragon Mountain, in Austria. What *was* the pile? An altar? A place of sacrifice? Did the Neanderthal men worship the great bears they hunted and put the skulls in this place as an act of respect? Or were the bear skulls put there as a sacrifice of thanksgiving to a god that had helped the Neanderthals have a successful hunt? We shall probably never know, but it is certain that cave bears were of great importance to the Neanderthal people, both as a source of food and as objects of some strange religious or magical ceremony.

The great cave bear hunted by our Neanderthal ancestors has a relative that looks very much like it living today. It is the North American grizzly bear. In fact, skeletons of the prehistoric cave bear and the modern grizzly are so much alike that many experts think the grizzly is the cave bear's descendant. It is believed that the grizzly's cave bear ancestors might have come to North America at the same time as the ancestors of the Indians, traveling across the bridge of land that connected North America and Asia during the late Ice Age.

Sadly enough, this beast that is so much like its prehistoric ancestor may soon be just as extinct as most of the long-ago mammals of the Ice Age. For the grizzly bear is vanishing. Where there once were hundreds of thousands of grizzlies, there are now probably less than 20 thousand, and their numbers grow less each year. So one of the last links with the prehistoric world that can still be seen and studied is following the saber-toothed cat and the mammoth down the road that leads to extinction.

Pronunciation Guide

The Mammals   Pages 60 to 91

Ankylosaurus	(ANG-kih-loh-SAW-ruhs)
Brontotherium	(BRAHN-toh-THEE-rih-uhm)
Diatryma	(DY-uh-TRY-muh)
Doedicurus	(dee-DIH-kyu-ruhs)
Edentate	(ee-DEN-tayt)
Eohippus	(EE-oh-HIP-uhs)
Glyptodon	(GLIP-toh-dahn)
Hyracotherium	(HY-ruh-koh-THEE-rih-uhm)
Icthyornis	(ik-thee-AWR-nehs)
Mammoth	(MAM-uhth)
Megatherium	(MEG-uh-THEE-rih-uhm)
Merychippus	(MER-ih-KIP-uhs)
Mesohippus	(MES-oh-HIP-uhs)
Neanderthal	(nee-AN-der-thahl)
Orohippus	(AWR-oh-HIP-uhs)
Oxyeana	(ahx-ee-EE-nuh)
Poëbrotherium	(POH-uh-broh-THEE-rih-uhm)
Smilodon	(SMY-loh-dahn)
Titanotherium	(TY-tan-oh-THEE-rih-uhm)
Toxodon	(TAHK-soh-dahn)

Index